The
Lord's Prayer
and
Rudolf Steiner

Also by Peter Selg

The Origins of the Creed of
The Christian Community

Rudolf Steiner and The Christian Community

Karl König's Path into Anthroposophy
Reflections from his Diaries
Karl König Archive, Volume 3

Ita Wegman and Karl König
Letters and Documents
Karl König Archive, Volume 2

The Lord's Prayer *and* Rudolf Steiner

A study of his insights into the archetypal
prayer of Christianity

Peter Selg

Floris
Books

Translated by Matthew Barton

First published in German as
Das Vaterunser in der Darstellung Rudolf Steiners
by Verlag Freies Geistesleben, Stuttgart in 2009
First published in English by Floris Books, Edinburgh in 2014
Third printing 2024
© 2009 Verlag Freies Geistesleben & Urachhaus GmbH
English version © 2014 Floris Books

British Library CIP Data available
ISBN 978-178250-051-3

Contents

Introduction   9

1. Respect for this Prayer   14
   The Lord's Prayer in Rudolf Steiner's Biography

2. Lord, Teach us to Pray   33
   Christ and the Disciples

3. Having the Courage to Invoke the
   Name of the Father   52
   The Lord's Prayer in Early Christianity

4. A Dialogue with the Divine   72
   The Inner Space of a 'Thought Mantra'

Notes   98

Bibliography   114

In memory of Friedrich Rittelmeyer

Where not otherwise indicated, all Gospel texts are taken from the Revised Standard Version of the Bible. Quotations followed by 'M' are from *The New Testament, a rendering* by Jon Madsen, Floris Books 1994.

Where the endnotes are more than textual references the endnote number is followed by an asterisk (*).

Introduction

The words of revelation call every era into their service. That a former time has said things of grandeur does not free the present time from its duty to make its own contribution.

Romano Guardini[1]

Thomas Aquinas called the Lord's Prayer 'the pre-eminent prayer' of Christendom, and Rudolf Steiner spoke of it as a key and central prayer of Christian experience, not only one of the world's 'profoundest prayers' but also of eminent importance for anthroposophically oriented meditation.[2] He once even called it the 'greatest initiation prayer'.[3] If we study Rudolf Steiner's biography, his spiritual stature and his work, there is no doubt at all that he lived intensively with the Lord's Prayer.

The Lord's Prayer is of very special worth. Christ not only gave it to his disciples and impressed its words intently upon them, but he himself was the first to speak it. Theological thought has had much to say about the Lord's Prayer throughout Christian history, including reflections on why the name of Christ himself does not appear anywhere in it although Christ Jesus is the core of all Christian confession. Here, however, it is of key importance to understand that Christ spoke the prayer for his disciples, including them, the inner core of the community, in his relationship with the Father.[4] The 'Our Father' in the Lord's Prayer relates to the Jordan Baptism and the voice heard then: 'Thou art my beloved son; today I have begotten thee.' (Luke 3:22 alternative reading). Paracelsus wrote: 'At the hour of Christ's birth, the name Father took its beginning, and before this had never been.'[5]

9

As their three years together unfolded, Christ eventually referred to his disciples as friends and brothers; yet in the Lord's Prayer, given to the disciples at an early stage, he had already united with them in the initial 'we' of Our Father.[6] In the High Priestly Prayer on Maundy Thursday, directly preceding the events of Gethsemane and Golgotha, he asked the Father to stand by the community of disciples in their fraternity with him: 'Father, I desire that they also, whom thou hast given me, may be with me where I am, to behold my glory which thou hast given me in thy love for me before the foundation of the world' (John 17:24). Christ spoke of and to his Father. After the Resurrection he spoke of 'My Father and your Father' (John 20:17).[7] In this context, praying the Lord's Prayer signifies entering into a form of words that Christ once formulated in his relationship to the Father, and in which he included the disciples in a decided way as friends and brothers. In certain respects, praying the Lord's Prayer is to pray in and with Christ, also in the meaning of John's phrase, 'If a man love me, he will keep my words: and my Father will love him, and we will come unto him, and make our abode with him' (John 14:23). Thomas Aquinas once spoke of how Christ, who gave the disciples the Lord's Prayer by praying it with them as their teacher, will hearken to it 'in community with the Father'.[8]

Whatever one may think about this, it seems of primary importance to acquire a sense that the 'prayer of Christ's disciples' is and remains intimately connected with Christ, and that he included the disciples in his words to the Father. Paul, in a future-oriented stance, wrote, 'It is no longer I who live; but Christ lives in me' (Gal.2:20). Rudolf Steiner referred to this in many contexts in relation to the development of the true, higher 'I'. In the view of Wilhelm Kelber, one of the founding priests of the Christian Community, these Pauline words relate as follows to the Lord's Prayer:

Christ exists where God's sonship or son nature arises in the soul, where the human I experiences and recognizes itself as son of the cosmic Father. As the 'Son of God', Christ is the brother of this I. As 'Son of Man' he signifies the human being's further evolution beyond himself, a state that comes about with the emergence of God's sonship ... The name Christ does not appear in the Lord's Prayer. This would make Christ into the object or recipient of the prayer, and thus he would be distanced from the inner soul. But precisely through the Lord's Prayer, Christ seeks to adopt a different place between human beings and the cosmic Father. He himself is the secret messenger of the Lord's Prayer in the soul. The Lord's Prayer is his means to indwell the human being.[9]

Karl Friedrich Althoff, a noted German philologist, Christologist and author, spoke tellingly of a prayer that 'consecrates the human being'.[10]

★

In the general Christological context outlined so far, with its premises and particular emphases, the current study seeks to illumine for modern readers Rudolf Steiner's contributions to a spiritual understanding of the Lord's Prayer. In a lecture he gave in 1907, over a century ago now, Rudolf Steiner said: 'Only in our day is it possible once again to extract from prayer what Christ imparted to it, and once again to know what power he invested especially into the Lord's Prayer.'[11] We know that Steiner's approach was neither theological nor based on textual exegesis or hermeneutics. Instead, he drew on original spiritual research, the nature of which still remains hidden and incomprehensible to many people today, and has frequently been the object of disparagement, mockery or ironic dismissal. Steiner's various statements on the Lord's Prayer are little known outside of anthroposophical circles. Yet even amongst those who take Rudolf Steiner's science of the spirit to heart, the scope, differentiation and depth of these statements is frequently overlooked or ignored. In this situation it seemed to me that addressing these themes within Rudolf Steiner's work and – at least in outline – presenting them anew, could offer a useful way forward. As in my previous study on Rudolf Steiner's accounts of the Jordan baptism and the Feast of Epiphany, these reflections will be complemented by the testimonies of early Christians.

Speaking to theologians, Rudolf Steiner once intimated that it is helpful to call to mind the feelings 'that early Christians experienced when hearing the Lord's Prayer or bringing it to life within them'.[12] It is not easy to do this, but not entirely impossible either – and Steiner himself repeatedly spoke of the importance of attempting it: 'Nowadays ... humanity must definitely summon up once more a spiritual engagement with Christianity such as that practised during early Christian centuries.'[13] Undertaking this kind of recall is not an end in itself but sharpens our awareness of the future-oriented content of esoteric Christianity, which in ecclesiastical tradition is often distorted beyond recognition and trivialized. Even the Lord's Prayer itself is not safe from such distortions.

At the beginning of the twentieth century, Rudolf Steiner opened up the source of esoteric Christianity in a new, yet methodical way, with extraordinary immediacy and clarity of intent. He did so both for individuals and the wider community. At the request of theologians, he also made it possible to reinstate a Christian ritual dedicated to the mystery character of the true Mass, in which the Lord's Prayer was reinvested with its central position and dignity. Christ gave the prayer to his disciples for the sanctity and seclusion of their inner life ('But when you pray, go into your room and shut the door and pray to your Father who is in secret; and your Father who sees in secret will reward you,' Matt.6:6). Yet at the same time he gave this prayer to the disciples as a community, and placed the words 'Our

Father' at the beginning. According to Luke, he gave the prayer when requested by a single disciple, who did so on behalf of the community: 'Lord, teach us to pray' (Luke 11:1). In this tension, or developmental moment, between the individual's inner path and the future tasks of the community – which, in the esoteric Christian sense also is or can be a community of worship – the Lord's Prayer took its way through the ages and cultures, and continues to do so today. Rudolf Steiner contributed to its progress on this path in significant ways. Let us hope that in future his input will be seen, valued and taken up to a greater degree than hitherto.

This short study is dedicated to Friedrich Rittelmeyer (1870–1938), an important theologian and co-founder of the Christian Community who worked alongside Rudolf Steiner, and whose important early studies on the Lord's Prayer were founded on his own inner experience of a Johannine practice of praying.

Peter Selg

1. Respect for this Prayer

The Lord's Prayer in
Rudolf Steiner's Biography

I grew up in a family of freethinkers, and my studies, too, led me toward freethinking. My own education was completely rooted in science.

Rudolf Steiner[1]

It does not seem at all likely that Rudolf Steiner ever heard the Lord's Prayer at home when he was growing up. At the end of 1913 he stressed that he never received any 'real Christian upbringing'.[2] His father, Johann, who ruled the household, was a freethinker and had little time for religion. After his childhood and youth, when he lived in the vicinity of a Premonstratensian Order (also known as 'White Canons'), he maintained as much distance as possible from the Church. Though Johann would speak with certain priests, he kept himself and his children at one remove.[3] In an autobiographical sketch, Steiner said that a 'certain natural indifference' toward religious tradition amongst his family and in the atmosphere of his early childhood 'they did not really bother with it.'[4] Besides christenings, the family did not attend church services together, and Steiner never mentioned people praying in his childhood home.

Despite this, Rudolf Steiner very probably encountered the Lord's Prayer during worship in church in the middle of his childhood, around the age of nine. Like his school friends he was an altar server at this time in Neudörfl an der Leitha, a small, one-street village south of Vienna. The family lived in the railway station premises outside the village, far from all friends. But Rudolf Steiner spent time with his peers at school and in church-related activities. At the end of his life he wrote of this time:

> The proximity of the church, and the graveyard around it, were deeply significant for me in my boyhood ... We schoolboys had to serve at the altar and sing in the choir at Mass, funerals and obsequies. The festive atmosphere of the Latin language and the service was an element which drew me strongly as a boy.

The Lord's Prayer doubtless was spoken on these occasions.[5]★ Despite Rudolf Steiner's scientific studies at the Technical College in Vienna, and his 'purely scientific' education, during which he engaged with materialistic positivism and contemporary epistemology, the Catholic clergy kept crossing his path. At the age of 25, he became acquainted with the Cistercian Father and Catholic polymath Wilhelm Anton Neumann, with whom – in a group of friends around the poet Marie Eugenie delle Grazie – he regularly held conversations.[6] We do not know whether Steiner occasionally attended Mass at the important Cistercian abbeys of Heiligkreuz, where Father Neumann lived, or Lilienfeld, close to Vienna. Quite other things were in the forefront of his life, work and encounters for many years; and he clearly voiced the same critique of ecclesiastical Christianity that his father had propounded before him.[7] Nevertheless, he retained a keen interest in the spiritual core of Christianity.

In Weimar, besides studying Goethe and Nietzsche, Steiner also engaged with Christian medieval philosophy, and in November 1900 gave an address on Thomas Aquinas to the Giordano Bruno Association in Berlin.[8] The theosophical lectures he began to give at the same period had a marked

Christian orientation. At this time, the autumn of 1900, he was 40 and by then, in the intimate seclusion of his inner life (of which little is known) had undergone rich and profound experiences relating to the Christ event. 'The important thing in my soul development was to have stood in spirit before the Mystery of Golgotha in inmost solemnity of festive insight,' he intimated in his autobiography.[9] After long trials, Rudolf Steiner was now willing to become a teacher in the Theosophical Society, and to act as General Secretary of its German section. He was not, however, prepared to represent or further its eastern outlook, which was far removed from Christianity. In a recollection of the early 1900s, and of conversations with Steiner, Marie Steiner-von-Sivers wrote:

> He could never, he said, do anything other than point to the difference between the two spiritual paths, and to the need for pursuing an occidental path of self-development. Merely gazing back to ancient wisdom was not feasible, without also including all intellectual capacities acquired since then and using them to progress upon the path of spiritual development in harmony with historical realities. The wisdom of the Orient, he said, was worthy of all admiration, and we should seek to fully understand it, while remembering that it does not substantially possess the element of progressive historical development which the Occident must now contribute. He regarded this as the task facing him, he said. The focus of his work, as he saw it, was the Mystery of Golgotha whose importance had not been acknowledged by the Orient and by movements that looked to it. I often heard him say such things, as early as the autumn of 1900, whenever eager theosophists pressed him on it. Anyone who heard the determination in these words knew that they expressed an unbendable will and historical necessity.[10]★

From the outset Marie von Sivers was a strong supporter of Rudolf Steiner's anthroposophical lectures and teaching activities, starting with the Berlin courses Mysticism at the Dawn of the Modern Age (winter 1900/1901) and Christianity as Mystical Fact (winter 1901/2). Steiner gave theosophical spiritual science a Christ-centric focus, placing it in the context of western cultural and spiritual history, despite meeting with only limited understanding for this approach from the theosophists.[11]* However, even Marie von Sivers failed to understand his sporadic engagement with Catholic clerics and interest in the Christian Mass. In her own childhood and youth, as the daughter of a major-general in Russian service in St Petersburg, she never encountered a Cistercian of the calibre of Father Neumann. It was in theosophy, and not in the Church, that she eventually found a way forward. During their first trip together to Italy at the end of 1906, however, Steiner wished to attend a midnight Christmas Mass at St Mark's Cathedral. He found the door closed, since Mass was no longer held there at this key moment in the year. Von Sivers wrote of this to the theosophist Edouard Schuré: 'We heard the midnight bells, but no single church was open, though no one had forbidden these priests from holding Mass.'[12] Her dismissal of the Catholic clergy in Venice came to further clear expression in the same letter:

> Sad, sad are the churches when the solemnity of their architecture is destroyed by the priests' small-minded behaviour. It is as if they retreat from their real tasks – which they no longer understand – in little backward steps, wrapping their priestly garb around them ineptly like a woman's dress. We saw the patriarch of Venice gesticulating, and speaking with exaggerated diction – as if a second-rate Italian actor were to relate the history of a long love affair with all the temperament of his race.

Rudolf Steiner very probably shared Marie von Sivers's view

of this – she wrote in the first person plural. Unlike her, though, Steiner did not regard Christian worship and its clergy as a lost cause. In the same letter to Schuré she wrote:

> I am glad, when all is said and done, that Dr Steiner in this life has seen a little of his old Italy.[13] And I will do all I can to arrange a month's incognito vacation for him in Rome next year, so that he can see for himself, more clearly than would be possible anywhere else, what his attitude must be to a Catholicism in decline.

Rudolf Steiner and Marie von Sivers did go to Rome in the summer of 1907, and in many subsequent years. Yet Rudolf Steiner changed his 'attitude to a Catholicism in decline' only to a very limited extent, and he enjoyed holding conversations with some of the clerics there and occasionally attending Mass. Rudolf Steiner not only stayed in the Catholic Church, which he had joined by christening shortly after his birth, but also kept a careful watch on the fate of Christianity (and thus also the Christian Church) although (or precisely because) he too was very aware of the signs of decline. Edouard Schuré replied to Marie von Sivers's Venice letter on January 24, 1907, writing:

> The old edifice of the Roman-Catholic religion must collapse from top to bottom to allow a more human and universal religion to take shape. But it seems to me that, as this broadens, it will again take up the major ideas and rites of Christianity, enlivening them with new inspiration.[14]

Schuré was close to the mark here. Just four days later, on January 28, 1907, in a talk given to members of the Theosophical Society in Berlin, Rudolf Steiner for the first time spoke of the Lord's Prayer, devoting the whole lecture to this theme.

★

Intended as 'an esoteric exegesis of the Lord's Prayer,' Rudolf Steiner explored the question of Christian prayer, its distinctive nature and specific meaning.[15] This was presented in the context of numerous reflections on the mysteries of Christianity, which Steiner embarked on during this period.[16] The anthroposophical foundations of religion were at the core of these lectures, which formed part of a continuum of western Christian esoteric thinking, as Steiner explicitly emphasized on January 28, 1907 in Berlin. In this vein he turned his attention to the Lord's Prayer at the beginning of a year during which he separated his esoteric school from the esoteric school of the Theosophical Society and faced his pupils with a decision about which path of spiritual development they wished to follow.[17] The esoteric school he directed and was responsible for, was one Steiner described as dedicated solely to the Christian and Christian-Rosicrucian path. The lecture on the Lord's Prayer in Berlin (which was followed by similar discourses in various cities) was released for publication by Steiner in July 1907. He mentioned it on various occasions – just four weeks after the two esoteric schools split from each other. Soon after this, in the autumn of 1907, he wrote as follows about the situation of the Theosophical Society to Edouard Schuré:

> Whether it [the Theosophical Society] will thrive and
> prosper in western lands depends on the extent to which
> it proves capable of including amongst its influences
> the principle of western initiation. You see, eastern
> forms of initiation must inevitably stop short before the
> Christ principle as central cosmic factor in evolution.
> Yet without this principle, the theosophical movement
> will be unable to exert any governing influence on
> western cultures, which are founded on Christ's life.
> The revelations of oriental initiation, on their own, can

only appear as a sectarian adjunct to a living western culture. They could only hope to prevail in evolution by eradicating the Christ principle from this western culture. Yet this would be tantamount to extinguishing the real purpose of the earth, which is embodied in insight into and realization of the intentions of the living Christ. To unveil these in their full wisdom, beauty and deed, however, is the deepest aim of Rosicrucianism. No one can deny that study of eastern wisdom is of the very greatest value since, while western people lost their sense of esoteric realities, this was preserved by eastern lands. But introduction of a fitting esotericism in the West must inevitably draw solely on the Rosicrucian-Christian path, since this is also what gave birth to western modes of life; and because its loss would deprive humanity of its meaning and purpose. Only in this realm of esotericism can a harmony arise between science and religion.[18]

In subsequent years, Rudolf Steiner repeatedly spoke of Christian Rosenkreutz, whose being he saw as intimately connected with both the preparation for and enactment of the events at the time of Christ.[19] He gave major lecture cycles on the Gospels and at the beginning of 1910, in a public lecture in Berlin entitled 'The Nature of Prayer,' he elaborated the inner conditions and factors involved in Christian prayer. According to Steiner, it was a matter of reassessing prayer, which within both Catholic and Protestant services had largely been distorted for egotistical purposes and distanced from its original nature. It was necessary, he said, to seek the real power of prayer in the human soul and acknowledge its reality. In striking terms, Steiner examined the anthropological basis of prayer in the temporal framework of human existence, elaborating how we can gain access to the divine, spiritual I in its actual developmental potency in human life in the past, present and future.[20]

At the very beginning of his lecture Steiner distinguished

the path of prayer from that of both mystic contemplation and spiritual-scientific research, but left no doubt that transitions exist between these three realms of activity of the human spirit-soul and that engaging in them depends on key preconditions. Rudolf Steiner spoke as a person of deep experience and familiarity with these matters – as someone who had practised them for many years.[21]

> If we strengthen our life of spirit in this way through prayer, then we need only await the effects, which will certainly become apparent. But only someone who has himself first perceived the power of prayer as reality will seek its effects in the outer world. Those who recognize this reality can try the following experiment. Having spurned the power of prayer for ten years, look back upon this ten-year period during which prayer has not figured in your life; then also look back upon a second ten-year period during which you did perceive the power of prayer. Then compare these two periods. You will see how the course of your life has changed under the sway of the power that you have imbued your soul with through prayer. Powers reveal themselves in their effects. It is easy to deny powers if one never calls forth their effects. How can anyone have the right to deny the power of prayer without ever having tried to actively invoke it within himself! ... We can only perceive a power that is to work in and through the soul by invoking and using it.[22]

In his lecture in relation to the Lord's Prayer, Steiner stated, among other things, that this prayer could also be a subject of meditation, and thus the focus of a genuine spiritual-scientific path of schooling:

> But however lofty a stage one may have attained, one has never finished working with a prayer, for it can always

raise the soul to a higher level. And the Lord's Prayer is a prayer that not only can be prayed but can also invoke a mystic mood, and can also be the object of higher meditation and concentration.[23]

In his lectures on the Lord's Prayer three years previously, Rudolf Steiner had already emphasized that Christian prayer (and in particular the Lord's Prayer) could acquire a meditative quality in 'a truly prayerful mood' in which one brings oneself into accord with divine will without an egotistic colouring of personal desire:

> If this mood of soul and sensibility is achieved as a truly prayerful mood, then Christian prayer is exactly the same as meditation – but just with a greater colouring of feeling quality. Originally Christian prayer was nothing other than meditation. Meditation involves a greater accentuation of thought, and through it one tries to attain harmony with the divine currents that flow through the world, by thinking of the great guide and helper of humanity. In prayer we can achieve the same thing in a more feeling way.[24]

For this reason, the Lord's Prayer played a certain role, too, in Steiner's esoteric school, although – according to his own words – it is not a mantra in the classical sense.[25]

> It is not an actual mantra, although it can have mantric powers. It is a thought mantra. Naturally it had the greatest power in its original language. But since it is a thought mantra, it will not lose its potency even if translated into a thousand different languages ... The content of thought in it is so mighty that it will not suffer diminution in any language.[26]

Rudolf Steiner showed how the Lord's Prayer can become the content of the most profound meditation. In a lesson of the esoteric school on February 6, 1910, shortly before the lecture in Berlin on the nature of prayer, Rudolf Steiner said:

> The Lord's Prayer, this wonderful reflection of the sevenfold principle of the world, is a meditation of great significance, which some pupils work with every day. I know of one of those whom we call the Masters of Wisdom and of the Harmony of Feelings, who stated: 'I meditate on the Lord 's Prayer only once a month; the rest of the time I try to make myself ripe and worthy to contemplate even just one phrase of this wonderful meditation.' This is how one should relate spiritually to a meditation – desiring to make oneself worthy enough to use it.[27]

Rudolf Steiner himself prayed the Lord's Prayer often and sometimes also loudly: in Berlin, neighbours in the building next door to 17 Motzstrasse, where he lived, could hear him praying it.[28]★ The transcript of a lecture he gave in 1907 reads: 'We should pray the Lord's Prayer, and do so every day.'[29] Answering questions on the Lord's Prayer after a lecture in Oslo in June 1912 he also said, however:

> One's respect for this prayer increases as one grows into it. There are ... times when, because of this prayer's lofty and exalted nature, one does not dare permit oneself to pray the whole Lord's Prayer on one day. One gains such a grandiose picture of the interplay of the seven petitions that one does not regard oneself as being worthy to unfold this greatest of initiation prayers in one's heart every day.[30]

★

When the First World War started in September 1914, Rudolf Steiner ceased his lecture cycles on the Gospels and Christological themes, and also the lessons of his esoteric school. But he did not stop pursuing his own esoteric work. During the war years he went on building the first Goetheanum in Dornach, stated his views of contemporary events in writing and talks, and often spoke about the dead and of ways to inwardly accompany them. In this context he did not speak further of the Lord's Prayer – or at least not in lectures of which transcripts are extant. Some of his pupils later gave striking accounts of the importance of the Lord's Prayer for the dead.[31]

After the war, likewise, Steiner did not again directly address Christological themes, although Friedrich Rittelmeyer requested – as he had done already during the war – that Steiner continue his lectures on the Fifth Gospel. ('During the World War, Dr Steiner's answer to me was that the "astral world" – the whole spiritual atmosphere around the earth – was now too troubled for him to be able to make investigations of this kind. After the war he said that other work was more pressing for humanity at the moment.'[32]) At that point, the focus of Steiner's efforts was on social threefolding initiatives and the re-enlivening of various professions (such as education and medicine) with the aid of anthroposophy. The 'Word' of modern spiritual science needed to become active in shaping civilization. Here, in the realm of social and scientific work, Steiner wanted an authentically Christian impulse to break through and take effect. Lectures on particular Christological themes now had to take a back seat in favour of realizing actual deeds. Yet the Lord's Prayer repeatedly figured in such endeavours.

Shortly after the Stuttgart Waldorf School opened, a member of the college of teachers asked Rudolf Steiner, during a meeting, about a morning verse for the children at the start of lessons.[33] [Generally German schools had a closer relationship to Christian religious practice than is the case in countries outside Europe]. In the next two days, Rudolf Steiner brought the teachers verses he himself had written for the start of lessons in the lower school and for pupils from Class Five upwards, and expressed his agreement with one teacher's proposal to begin lessons by saying the Lord's Prayer: 'I would think it a very fine thing to start lessons with the Lord's Prayer. Then you can continue with the verses that I will give you.'[34] But while the verses Steiner gave came to be spoken at the beginning of each morning in the Waldorf School, the same was not done with the Lord's Prayer for reasons that have not been recorded. Despite invariably stressing the school's freedom from any religious or philosophical bias, Steiner himself would have welcomed a school day that began in this fashion.

In a difficult pedagogical situation (after it became necessary to start a new class when two parallel classes grew too big) Steiner recommended saying the Lord's Prayer at the beginning of the day, with pronounced success. According to the new teacher, Martha Haebler, not only did he oversee the reconfiguration of the class and personally introduce the children to their new teacher, but also suggested she use the Lord's Prayer, to accompany this new beginning, most probably to support the newly forming class community: 'Now I stood before the class to speak the familiar morning verse, "I look into the world," but before I could follow this with a song, he urged us to speak the Lord's Prayer together, and this was something we continued to do throughout the following years.'[35]

Steiner likewise spoke about the Lord's Prayer in an English lesson in a different class. Rudolf Treichler, the teacher, described this unusual situation as follows:

> On one occasion, when I was teaching English to a
> Class Eight, I began – as I have since continued to do
> in all middle school classes – to study the Lord's Prayer
> with the children, in that resonant, antiquated English
> that still lives today in the King James Bible. Dr Steiner

entered the classroom and, taking a seat, listened to us quietly with his usual friendly attentiveness. I spoke the prayer aloud and the pupils spoke it after me; and after the final words had been spoken – For thine is the kingdom, the power and the glory, Amen – suddenly and unexpectedly Dr Steiner got up and went to the board with lively energy, picked up the chalk and said, 'Dear children, you all know what a kingdom is, and that it is of a certain size and breadth, which we can draw like this,' he drew a circle. 'And you also know that the king in his might usually has his seat and centre in the middle of his realm, from where his whole power emanates to the outermost boundaries of his kingdom,' he pointed to the middle of the circle and indicated a few radial lines. 'But his glory and magnificence extend far beyond these boundaries,' he indicated around the circle by flowing rays and lines. 'And the whole gives us the picture of?' he asked.

'The sun' replied all the children joyfully and fully involved.

'Yes, that is the picture of the sun,' said Dr Steiner brightly and benevolently. He took his leave of us with a loving smile, shook hands with me, and left. It really seemed to all of us as if a bright gleam remained behind in the classroom. We left the drawing on the board for a long, long time; and even when it was finally erased, it continued to illumine our shared prayer to the Father.[36]

Thus the Lord's Prayer was present in diverse ways in the Stuttgart Waldorf School under Rudolf Steiner's auspices in the years following the First World War, even though it was not an intrinsic part of the usual morning verse.

★

Three years after the Waldorf school opened, the Christian Community, was founded in the autumn of 1922 at the initiative of some young theology students and ministers of religion who were involved with anthroposophy.[37] Rudolf Steiner helped the theologians in every way, just as he stood by the teachers at the Stuttgart school. The words of the rituals – or, in Edouard Schuré's words, the 'major ideas and rites of Christianity' – were newly formulated by Steiner for this new movement in accord with contemporary spiritual circumstances, which Steiner described as an 'age of light'. In this context he also highlighted the meaning, value and place of the Lord's Prayer within the Christian Mass. In a lecture about the elements of the new rites, given to the group of theologians on September 11, 1922, he said:

> All denominations have grown very lax in relation to the Lord's Prayer in our times. The Lord's Prayer was originally a kind of compendium of the most important truths of the cosmos, as mirrored in human feeling. In Protestantism, the Lord's Prayer, I would say, is not always spoken in a way that is prepared with sufficient care. Just consider the solemn, ceremonial quality involved in speaking it after the Transubstantiation has been accomplished, and how the Lord's Prayer comes at this particular point (before communion). This does not mean that a person of faith ought not to pray the Lord's Prayer as often as possible. But even the simplest individual prayer, such as the Lord's Prayer, is prayed in a more worthy way in Roman Catholicism due to the fact that the faithful hear it at a key juncture in the Mass. This prepares the whole mood in which the Lord's Prayer is spoken – a certain ceremonial nuance.
>
> However, the Catholic Church has succeeded in eradicating this ceremonial nuance in its adherents at Confession, when the priest hearing Confession tells the penitent to pray five Lord's Prayers every day. This

bartering of sin against the Lord's Prayer is of course a dreadful thing and removes all the sanctity the Lord's Prayer acquires when it is spoken during the Mass, where it always retains this fundamentally ceremonial and solemn tone. What the Catholic Church also achieves in this respect by holding Mass in Latin – which is after all incomprehensible to the faithful – can be replaced by the power with which you can recite the Lord's Prayer during Mass; for just reciting the Lord's Prayer does not really accord with its intrinsically majestic quality. Though I do not in any way wish to suggest that we should undertake something with the slightest air of magic about it – something the Catholic Church achieves through the Latin language – it must nevertheless be said that in a certain respect the Latin language can also subtly invoke profound truths in the Lord's Prayer, truths that should never be trivialized, even in the absence of any magical dimension. There is in fact a certain justification in the fact that Latin continued to be used for so long, with the aim of leading humanity beyond the merely personal realm. But today, what this speaking of the Lord's Prayer before the congregation in Latin achieved must be replaced by the power with which it is spoken. During an act of worship, a person of faith must hear the Lord's Prayer – precisely because it is his daily prayer – in a way that is raised beyond the usual mode of speech. In Latin, the Lord's Prayer is in a sense configured in a way that renders it a mantra:

Oremus. Praecepis salutaribus moniti et divina
institutione formati, audemus dicere:
Pater noster, qui es in coelis:
sanctificetur nomen tuum:
adveniat regnum tuum:
fiat voluntas tua, sicut in coelo et in terra.
Panem nostrum quotidianum da nobis hodie,

et dimitte nobis debita nostra,
sicut et nos dimittimus debitoribus nostris.
Et ne os inducas in tentationem.
Sed libera nos a malo.

The mantric quality present in the Latin Lord's Prayer
must in turn pass over somewhat into the Lord's Prayer
when it is prayed at the point between Transubstantiation
and Communion.[38]

In his Berlin lecture in February 1910 on 'The Nature of
Prayer', twelve years before the Christian Community was
founded, Rudolf Steiner suggested the following:

To go into further details about the effects of prayer
(you will have to take my word for this) is really not
possible in our present times, however unprejudiced
one's view of these times may be. You see, as yet we lack
the elements in our contemporary outlook that would
allow people to understand that a communal prayer – that
is, the confluence of powers that arise from a praying
congregation – has an enhanced spiritual potency and
thus an enhanced power of reality. Today, therefore, we
will make do with what we have been considering here in
relation to the inner nature of prayer.[39]

When the Christian Community was founded, Rudolf Steiner
emphasized that, if a person prays without any attendant ritual,
a spiritual being must help that prayer to become full spiritual
reality.[40] Steiner gave substantial help so that the Lord's Prayer
could once again resound with full power before a congregation
in a new inspirationally enlivened (as Schuré said) Christian act of
worship. The priest alone was to pray aloud the Lord's Prayer as
part of the Act of Consecration of Man (the Communion service
of the Christian Community) between the Transubstantiation and

Communion while the congregation should pray it inwardly with him, in the confluence of powers which Steiner refers to above.

★

The Lord's Prayer was by no means the 'new' cultural element in the pedagogy of the Stuttgart Waldorf School and in the Christian Community rituals, and yet it was an element in the spirit of both. In a sense this was also true for medicine, and thus for the triad of science, the arts of healing and education, and religion.[41]★ Rudolf Steiner did not focus on this original Christian prayer in any of his medical courses, although his mantric instruction for medical students and young physicians related to it (as did the core Foundation Stone meditation which was given at the Christmas Foundation Meeting[42]). But in collaborating with the physician Ita Wegman on a medical textbook of several volumes (the first volume of which was published as Fundamentals of Therapy), Steiner began their work each evening by speaking the Lord's Prayer aloud, standing. People passing outside the studio could hear him.[43] Despite his grave illness, Rudolf Steiner continued saying the Lord's Prayer in this way, standing, until his very last days.[44] The day before he died, having just written the introductory chapter of the medical book, he handed Ita Wegman the corrected manuscript and said, 'Significant things have been given in this book.'[45]

Rudolf Steiner likewise considered that the Lord's Prayer contained 'true knowledge of the human being' that was of significance in healing – and to the very end he lived in its spirit, mood and content. In his interpretations, Steiner described the heavenly powers in the first three petitions of the Lord's Prayer that can enable us to transform, illumine and Christianize the earthly realm. He drew on and worked out of this dimension in his life and work, right up to his last day on earth, in tireless commitment to a renewal of civilization at the very brink of the abyss of the twentieth century.

A particular blow to Steiner was the destruction of the First Goetheanum in an arson attack, an example of the evil that assailed his path, as it had that of the early Christians. But never for one moment did he give up. He continued to work out of that fundamental 'mood of prayer' which he had characterized in such incisive terms in Berlin in 1910. Steiner used many sacred texts and left behind an extensive collection of mantric works. Yet he himself lived to the end with and within Christ's prayer, regarding it as the loftiest of all.

It is not certain which precise wording of the Lord's Prayer Rudolf Steiner spoke in his studio in Dornach (and whether the version he prayed with Ita Wegman when they worked on the medical book was identical with that prayed during his illness).[46] Steiner had been much preoccupied with diverse translations of the prayer. The day after his first lecture on the Lord's Prayer of January 28, 1907 in Berlin, he said during an esoteric lesson: 'Spoken in German, the underlying thought is almost all that still takes effect. The effect is enhanced in the Latin Pater noster; but the prayer's whole power and fullness only come to expression in the original Aramaic.'[47]

Possibly at the request of certain individuals, Rudolf Steiner gave his own version of the Lord's Prayer to a small group of people. We do not have any further information about this text, different variants of which have been preserved. Nor do we know how it arose, or the precise date in the years before the First World War when it was written down (though not in Rudolf Steiner's own handwriting).[48] According to Marie Steiner-von Sivers, Steiner referred to it as the Esoteric Lord's Prayer or the Lord's Prayer of the Apostles.[49] The Old Catholic priest Hugo Schuster, who was a member of the esoteric school, was aware of this version of the prayer, and was known to have spoken it at a Catholic funeral in October 1920, in the presence of Rudolf Steiner.[50] Steiner had given Schuster his own wording for the funeral rites in the winter of 1918/19.[51]

Ita Wegman recorded the text of the Esoteric Lord's Prayer in one of her notebooks, and gave a copy of it to her sister, Charlien Hupkes, telling her that Rudolf Steiner had prayed this with her before they started work each day on the medical book.[52] It can therefore be assumed that this was the wording of the Esoteric Lord's Prayer spoken in the studio until their collaboration ended:[53]

Father, you who were, are, and will be in the inmost being of all of us!
May your name be glorified in us all and praised.
May your kingdom grow more expansive in our deeds and in the conduct of our lives.
May we enact your will in our life as you, Father, have enshrined it in our inmost heart and soul.
In overflowing abundance you give us spiritual nourishment, the bread of life, through all changing conditions of our lives.
Let our mercy toward others atone for the sins perpetrated upon our being.
You do not allow the tempter to work in us beyond the capacity of our strength – for no temptation can prevail in your being; and the tempter is only appearance and delusion, from which you will safely deliver us, Father, through the light of your knowledge.
May your power and glory work in us through all cycles of time.[54]★

2. Lord, Teach us to Pray
Christ and the Disciples

According to the Evangelist Matthew, Christ Jesus gave his disciples the Lord's Prayer in the first period of their association, on a mountain in Galilee, as part of a longer sequence of intimate instruction that later came to be known as the Sermon on the Mount. It was, however, no sermon in the modern sense. Karl Friedrich Althoff wrote:

> According to the Gospel of Matthew, at the lofty place of the Sermon on the Mount, Christ for the first time reveals in words his true being to the disciples. He entrusts them with completing his work, and teaches them to invoke in prayer, in the human soul, the hidden Father God as the cosmic ground of being. Christ establishes a new foundation for living, creating and perceiving through co-existence with one's neighbour as human brother in the presence of the opening world of God the Father. The Lord's Prayer occupies the compositional centre of these instructions. At the same time it stands at the centre of a new, threefold rationale of human existence: in our conduct towards our fellow human beings (forgiveness and mercy), in our relationship to the divine world (prayer) and towards ourselves (fasting).[1]

This instruction on the mountain preceded Christ's activity of preaching and healing in Galilee. Many people had followed him, but then Christ withdrew to the mountain accompanied only by his disciples. According to Matthew, he 'seated himself' and then his disciples 'came to him' (Matt.5:1) in a process of withdrawal, self-composure and concentration.[2]*

Rittelmeyer spoke of the Sermon on the Mount as a 'school of prayer'.[3] Precisely in the middle of his instruction, Christ spoke of the mode and path of prayer as a relationship with God that is capable of permeating a person's whole existence and actions:

Beware of practising your piety before men in order to be seen by them; for then you will have no reward from your Father who is in heaven.

Thus, when you give alms, sound no trumpet before you, as the hypocrites do in the synagogues and in the streets, that they may be praised by men. Truly, I say to you, they have received their reward. But when you give alms, do not let your left hand know what your right hand is doing, so that your alms may be in secret; and your Father who sees in secret will reward you.

And when you pray, you must not be like the hypocrites; for they love to stand and pray in the synagogues and at the street corners, that they may be seen by men. Truly, I say to you, they have received their reward. But when you pray, go into your room and shut the door and pray to your Father who is in secret; and your Father who sees in secret will reward you.

And in praying do not heap up empty phrases as the Gentiles do; for they think that they will be heard for their many words. Do not be like them, for your Father knows what you need before you ask him. Pray then like this:

Our Father who art in heaven,
Hallowed be thy name.
Thy kingdom come,
Thy will be done

On earth as it is in heaven.
Give us this day our daily bread.
And forgive us our debts
As we also have forgiven our debtors;
And lead us not into temptation,
But deliver us from evil.
For thine is the kingdom, and the power, and the glory,
forever.

Amen.

For if you forgive men their trespasses, your heavenly
Father also will forgive you; but if you do not forgive
men their trespasses, neither will your Father forgive your
trespasses. (Matt.6:1–15).

At a later point in his address to them, Christ told the disciples
that their prayer would be heard (or answered) if it were done
with the right inner stance: 'Ask, and it will be given you; seek,
and you will find; knock, and it will be opened to you. For
every one who asks receives, and he who seeks finds, and to
him who knocks it will be opened.' (Matt.7:7f). Even in human
conditions, he tells them, every father will give his son what the
latter asks for 'If you then, who are evil, know how to give good
gifts to your children, how much more will your Father who is
in heaven give good things to those who ask him' (Matt.7:11).

According to Matthew, those who heard the Sermon on the
Mount were 'astonished' (Matt.7:28). Rudolf Steiner regarded
it as the 'most important revelation of Christianity'.[4] An entirely
new perspective on human existence had opened up for them:
on life and moral conduct in a divinely created world; on the
'thou' nature of human life, both in relation to the ground of
being of Creation and to other human beings. The prayer to the
Father which Christ gave the community of disciples was the
core of this existential and radical teaching of authentic renewal:

'Therefore let this be your prayer.'

The evangelist Luke also testified to the entrusting of the Lord's Prayer to the disciples. According to Luke this occurred at a later point – after the return of the seventy disciples from their work of preaching and healing, and after the parable of the Good Samaritan and the time spent with Martha and Mary. Mary – whom Bock describes as 'the person of prayer and of sacramental reverence,' had seated herself at the feet of Christ Jesus and was attending to his words.[5]

> But Martha was distracted with much serving; and she went to him and said, 'Lord, do you not care that my sister has left me to serve alone? Tell her then to help me.' But the Lord answered her, 'Martha, Martha, you are anxious and troubled about many things; one thing is needful. Mary has chosen the good portion, which shall not be taken away from her.' (Luke 10:40–42).

Luke speaks further of this 'one' needful and vital thing in his words about the Lord's Prayer directly following on from the account of the meeting with Martha and Mary:

> Once, he was absorbed in prayer in a quiet place. And when he paused, one of his disciples said to him, 'Lord, teach us the way of prayer, as John also taught it to his disciples.' And he said to them, 'When you pray, say this:
>
> Father,
> may your name be hallowed,
> may your Kingdom come to us;
> give us each day our daily bread,
> forgive us our sins, as we forgive all those who are indebted to us,
> and lead us not into temptation. (Luke 11:1–4 M).

According to Luke, too, Christ acknowledges that this prayer will be heard ('Ask and it will be given you ...'). The heavenly Father, he says, will send the 'Holy Spirit' to those who ask for it (Luke 11:13).

★

In Luke's account, the giving of the Lord's Prayer occurred at the request of an unnamed disciple, following the disciples' witnessing of Christ praying, 'when he paused' in his prayer.[6]★ Christ Jesus often prayed to his Father. As Luke described, the three years of his work on earth began as follows:

> Now when all the people were baptized, and when Jesus also had been baptized and was praying, the heaven was opened, and the Holy Spirit descended upon him in bodily form, as a dove, and a voice came from heaven, 'Thou art my beloved Son; with thee I am well pleased.' (Luke 3:21f emphasis added)

The Gospel of John, in particular, points to Christ's continual stance of prayer, as Friedrich Rittelmeyer described:

> The Gospel of John is a window through which one can view Christ himself in his inner life. The background to all his outer life is an uninterrupted inner conversation with the Father ... The other evangelists also tell us in full clarity how Christ's life is born out of prayer and everywhere sustained by prayer, how it passes in pure prayer. But in the Gospel of John, Christ's continuous speech with the Father is something we can experience in the most intimate possible way.[7]

Christ's prayers at the grave of Lazarus, at the Last Supper, in the Garden of Gethsemane, and on the hill of Golgotha were reported (in fragments) by the disciples. Frequently, however, Christ Jesus withdrew and prayed alone: 'And in the morning, a great while before day, he rose and went out to a lonely place, and there he prayed' (Mark 1:35). 'And he withdrew into the wilderness, and prayed' (Luke 5:16). 'On one occasion he had withdrawn to devote himself completely to prayer' (Luke 9:18 M). 'And after he had dismissed the crowds, he went up on the mountain by himself to pray' (Matt.14:23). 'Jesus withdrew again to the mountain by himself' (John 6:15). Christ repeatedly withdrew to a 'mountain' – often the Mount of Olives – to pray. His transfiguration on Mount Tabor took place in full view of the disciples while Christ prayed ('And as he prayed, the fashion of his countenance was altered' Luke 9:29). Rudolf Frieling, in an unsurpassed study of Christ's withdrawals into the solitude of prayer wrote: 'while he prayed, and through the fact of praying, the process of transfiguration began.'[8] In Gethsemane, too, Christ withdrew, turning away from the last three disciples and praying to his Father.[9]

Thus only a few of his prayers were directly heard by the disciples and later recorded in the Gospels, and yet those within the inner circle around Christ were often near at hand to witness what happened. In prayer, Christ invoked his Father. He 'rested at the centre of his I-being' and sought to unite with the will of the divine Father before all important decisions and with his whole being ('not what I will, but what thou wilt' Mark 14:36).[10] Luke wrote of the way Christ called together the inner group of disciples: 'In these days he went out to the mountain to pray; and all night he continued in prayer to God. And when it was day, he called his disciples, and chose from them twelve, whom he named apostles.' (Luke 6:12f). From his inward contemplation during nightly prayer, he chose and called together the twelve in the morning.

In accomplishing his acts of healing, likewise, Christ turned his gaze upwards to the Father (Mark 7:34). On the Cross, too, he prayed for his enemies in the spirit of the Sermon on the

Mount ('But I say to you, Love your enemies and pray for those who persecute you, so that you may be sons of your Father who is in heaven; for he makes his sun rise on the evil and on the good, and sends rain on the just and on the unjust.' Matt.5:44f emphasis added). 'And when they came to the place which is called The Skull, there they crucified him, and the criminals, one on the right and one on the left. And Jesus said, "Father, forgive them; for they know not what they do".' (Luke 23:33f).

Christ Jesus sometimes prayed aloud in public situations; but often – much more often – in the quiet of a secluded place. As Matthew reports, Christ also urged the disciples to pray in seclusion before he gave them the Lord's Prayer. Althoff translated the relevant passage (into German).

> Whenever you pray, be not as showmen are; for these love to stand at gathering places (synagogues) and at street corners to pray. In this way they desire to be seen by people. Truly I say to you: they have their reward therein. But when you pray, go into your chamber, and having closed your door, call in prayer upon your Father, who dwells in seclusion. And your Father, whose gaze you will meet in seclusion, will endow you with gifts.[11]

According to Althoff, Christ withdrew prayer from the public domain of temple and synagogue worship and transferred it to 'the inmost nature of awakening selfhood,' into the 'little chamber' which is both the treasure or store chamber and also the I-organ of the human heart as Thomas Aquinas emphasized.[12] Christ respected the ancient place of divine worship and spoke as Isaiah did of the temple as a 'house of prayer' that should be kept sacred (Isa.56:7, Mark 11:17). But communion with God in prayer must be accomplished within the human I, irrespective of the physical location where this I is dwelling. In answer to the Samaritan woman who asked where the right place of prayer and worship could be found – at the shrine on Mount Gerizim or in the temple at Jerusalem – Christ replied that in future this distinction would no longer apply: 'But the hour is coming, and now is, when the true worshipers will worship the Father in spirit and truth, for such the Father seeks to worship him. God is spirit, and those who worship him must worship in spirit and truth.' (John 4:23f). Thus they must worship him irrespective of location.

Christ spoke of praying in living words of reality, in communion with the power of the Word – with his Logos nature. A prayer was not to contain 'empty words'. Althoff renders the spirit of the Greek text here as: 'Do not hack to pieces and shatter the power of the Logos (with your begging)!'[13]★ Christ spoke of the need for pure elevation, without the articulation of personal desires ('Do not be like them, for your Father knows what you need before you ask him.' Matt.6:8), and with a willingness to adopt a peaceful and forgiving stance towards the world. 'The person praying will only render his prayer real and effective when he bears peace within himself and creates peace with his surroundings.'[14]

Christ taught his disciples to address the Father – who was both his and theirs – in a new form of consciousness that was highly distinctive in character:

> Only one person – the high priest – among all the
> thousands of the nation's people, was allowed to speak
> this name of God [in the Old Testament], and only once
> a year on the great Day of Atonement. And he could do
> so only at one single place: the innermost shrine of the
> temple; and only under one condition: after atonement
> by the whole nation.[15]

In the High Priestly Prayer, Christ said of the disciples to his Father: 'I made known to them thy name, and I will make it known, that the love with which thou hast loved me may be in them, and I in them' (John 17:26). The Father who is invoked is 'in heaven' yet at the same time stands in relation to the human I. Aquinas explained this as follows:

> He [God] is very close to us. 'Who art in heaven' means, properly understood: in the holy ones; within whom lives God, (Jer.14:9: 'Thou, O Lord, art in the midst of us') ... Since some assert that God does not, due to his loftiness, concern himself with human things (Job 22:14: 'Thick clouds enwrap him, so that he does not see, and he walks on the vault of heaven') it must by contrast be emphasized that he is close to us, indeed, that he lives in our inmost ground of being.[16]

Thus invocation of the Father should occur out of this inmost ground of being and be intrinsically related to the petition to hallow or glorify the divine name in continuous consecration, opposing all tendency to misuse of it 'so that the holiness of God be perceived'.[17] In the Old Testament we read, 'And you shall not profane my holy name, but I will be hallowed among the people of Israel; I am the Lord who sanctify you' (Lev.22:32).

Christ taught the existence of the Father God, and of the coming kingdom, in relation to each individual's innermost being: not as external power and reality but as the self-realizing goal of every individual and the community as a whole. According to Luke (17:21), Christ said, 'behold, the kingdom of God is within you.' The kingdom of God – as the sphere of activity of the Son – has commenced and is growing: 'But if it is by the Spirit of God that I cast out demons, then the kingdom of God has come upon you' (Matt.12:28). The individual's inner growth and his petition to have a part in the kingdom of heaven ('Hold sway in our heart' as Aquinas said[18]) aims to invoke collaboration of the Christ-permeated human being in initiating what is to come and has already begun. In Matthew, Christ says to his disciples: 'Pray therefore the Lord of the harvest to send out laborers into his harvest. ' (Matt.9:38). These labourers are the disciples themselves who are to accomplish this work in an exemplary way. 'Whoever meditates upon this phrase in prayer (Thy kingdom come) can grow into the whole nature of the human being: What is to come will do so through the human being.'[19]

If, in this way, the kingdom of God enters the human I so that divine will penetrates the earthly sphere, the community of Christians prepares the earth's renewal and new being, its transformation through Christ. The disciples were the primary organ of Christ's activity as individuals and as a group, as archetype and exemplar of a future human community.[20] They were summoned to work at the earth's development both through teaching and healing, but also through the conduct of their own lives, and through their transformed relationship with the surrounding world, as 'salt of the earth' (Matt.5:13). Rittelmeyer wrote in his treatise on the Lord's Prayer:

> The third petition already speaks of the earth: Thy will be done on earth as it is in heaven. Thus divine will initially shines over the earth, which is joined to the heavens as their lowest aspect. The earth is consecrated as the locus where divine will should prevail: as it is in heaven.[21]

In engagement with the fruits of the earth, with every 'you', but also with the dangers of evil, the disciples are to pursue an exemplary path through their fraternity with Christ ('Blessed are the eyes which see what you see' Luke 10:23). The last four petitions of the Lord's Prayer refer to this path, the realization of the kingdom of God: his will and the hallowing of his name on earth.

Neither Matthew nor Luke relate any details about how the disciples continued to work with the Lord's Prayer. There is no record of how the prayer lived in the community and individuals, or whether the disciples prayed it together with Christ. But since the prayer was given and entrusted to them in a special way, it no doubt had central importance for them. Christ frequently returned to the subject of what had been given to the disciples, both obliquely and in express words. According to Luke, he prayed for Peter and the community in their battle with evil: 'Simon, Simon, see Satan is trying hard to get you all; he will shake you through the sieve just like wheat is sifted. For you, Simon, I have prayed, that your inner strength may not fail. When you have come to yourself again, you shall strengthen your brothers.' (Luke 22:31f M).[22] Even in Gethsemane Christ urged the disciples to take the sixth petition of their Lord's Prayer to heart: 'Watch and pray that you may not enter into temptation; the spirit indeed is willing, but the flesh is weak' (Mark 14:38). A few hours previously, after the Last Supper, he had petitioned his Father again on their behalf: 'I do not pray that thou shouldst take them out of the world, but that thou shouldst keep them from the evil one' (John 17:15). To the very end the disciples could witness in Christ how a life lived in the essence of the Lord's Prayer could unfold in a consistently authentic way, even if the last four human petitions were spoken not for himself but for them (and all people). He lived beyond guilt, temptation and evil, yet encountered these on earth, in the sphere of human life.

★

According to Rudolf Steiner's research, the giving of the Lord's Prayer to the disciples had long antecedents connected with the destiny of Jesus of Nazareth in the years before the baptism. In his lectures on the Fifth Gospel, Steiner described Jesus' inner path to the Jordan baptism and to John the Baptist as the preparation for the Christ's incarnation which initially occurred at the Jordan and then went on to determine the three years of Christ Jesus on earth. This was a process of intensifying union of the divine being with the physical body, culminating and concluding at Golgotha.[23] Jesus pursued this path with distinctive qualities derived from both the 'Nathan' and 'Solomon' lines.[24]

From his youth onwards Jesus underwent painful processes of development that brought home to him the decline and degeneration of old forms of spirituality that had previously informed and dictated human culture, and along with these, the threat of destruction for human souls. According to Steiner, he experienced the demise of ancient Jewish spiritual culture, which had lost its sources of inspiration and had rigidified into mere tradition. He also witnessed the decline of the pagan (Mithras) mysteries in Palestine and ultimately the failure of the Essenes, who acquired their purity only at the expense of others in a form of spiritual withdrawal which offered no progressive evolution to humanity.[25]

Jesus experienced the decline of the pagan mysteries (the second stage of his three-stage path of suffering preceding the event at the Jordan) in an especially dramatic way: he saw that demons had appropriated the ancient altars of the rites, exerting a destructive influence so that people fell ill. In his encounter with the fallen altar, the flight of the priests, the demons and people's suffering, Jesus was, according to Steiner, lifted out of himself and removed to 'the sphere of the sun' where he heard words that 'resounded as if from the spheres of sun existence'.[26] What Jesus perceived as inspiration in this exceptional state was, said Rudolf Steiner, 'the secret of primordial pagan revelation' or the 'ancient teachings of pagan humanity', the 'all-prevailing prayer' of ancient mystery rites whose definitive decline informed this whole situation. The content of this ancient prayer of the mysteries, said Steiner, was the 'secret of evolving humanity': condensed into mantric form, a teaching of human incarnation lived in the high spiritual cultures of ancient times and at the sites of their shrines and rites. The 'secret of the self-incorporating human being, descending from the macrocosm to the microcosm' or the 'secret of all human embodiment in physical, earthly corporeality' was known at these mystery centres, as was also, therefore, the human being's loss of his spiritual home in cosmic existence. On September 20, 1913,

Rudolf Steiner first presented the words of the 'all-prevailing prayer' of the ancient mystery centres, which Jesus of Nazareth had heard:

Amen
Evils hold sway
Witness to separating I-hood
Trespass of selfhood through others incurred
Experienced in daily bread
Wherein the will of heaven does not rule
Because man sundered himself from your realm
And forgot your names
You Fathers in the heavens.[27]

In former times, the mystery centres focused on the situation of the incarnated human being, knowing the dangers and evil connected with it, and in expectation of the turning point that they yearned for and awaited. Rudolf Steiner spoke of these mantric words as a 'prayer', and at the same time made clear that it could also become the subject of profound meditation in the contemporary world of the twentieth century:

> Since I have become aware of these words, I have found them to be an extraordinarily important formulation for meditation. They have a quite extraordinary power over the soul, and you can say that the more one reflects upon them, the more one notices the power these words have
> ...
> Increasingly, as I myself have discovered, in meditating repeatedly on these words, one comes to see the vast depths they contain.[28]

Rudolf Steiner does not say when and by what means he 'became aware' of these words of 'ancient pagan revelation'. He first spoke them on September 20, 1913, on the occasion of the laying of the foundation stone of the First Goetheanum in Dornach. These words were preceded by the 'AUM' of a primordial mystery mantra that he had already given as material for meditation to his esoteric pupils (including Ita Wegman) in the first decade of the twentieth century.[29] 'Descent from the spirit, life in the material world, and return to the spirit is embodied in three letters: AUM.'[30]

> I avow me to myself: ah
> I avow myself to humanity: u
> I avow myself to life: m[31]

★

The experiences of Jesus of Nazareth went further. He saw the necessity of a turning point in history, for a 'new spiritual impulse,' that would have to be able to change the course of humanity's destiny and redress its almost total separation from the world of spirit which had reached a nadir and was approaching catastrophic dimensions. 'What is to become of humanity when it succumbs to the fate of the individual?'[32] Jesus felt the need for a new beginning, one however, that could not emerge from the powers of ancient humanity but instead from a 'macrocosmic illumining of the earth'.[33] After long preparations, he finally became the bearer of this impulse through the baptism event: the macrocosmic Christ spirit entered him in a process that signified a 'conception' in the true sense.[34] Christ was received into the sphere of earth:

> The Fifth Gospel tells us that the words of the Luke
> Gospel are a true reflection of what could have
> been heard at that time if a developed, clairvoyant
> consciousness had hearkened to the cosmic expression of
> the mystery that was accomplished there. The words that
> resounded from heaven actually were: This is my much-

loved Son, whom today I have begotten. These are the
words of the Gospel of Luke, and are also a true reflection
of what occurred then: the begetting or conception of
Christ within the being of earth. This is what took place
at the Jordan.[35]

After this mighty transformation and in the discovery of a
new equilibrium within earthly existence, Christ Jesus spent
forty days in the wilderness where he encountered the dual
form of evil, including Ahriman, who urged him to turn stones
into bread.[36]* Largely vanquishing them, Christ Jesus left the
adversaries behind him. But he found Ahriman's influence at
work again among the human beings he next encountered:
labourers and publicans who in their hard lives were reliant
on turning 'stones into bread'. According to the Fifth Gospel,
this situation was new for Christ Jesus: he encountered it with
amazement, and, with great compassion and emphatic empathy,
commenced his work of healing. He taught and healed, liberating
many people from the powers that burdened them and dragged
them down, thus initiating a new impetus in evolution while
remaining aware of the 'all-prevailing prayer' of the old mystery
centres, whose earthly reality grew ever more apparent to him.

> ...
> Experienced in daily bread
> Wherein the will of heaven does not rule
> Because man sundered himself from your realm
> And forgot your names
> You Fathers in the heavens
> ...

Due to their destiny and earthly situation of embodiment and
materialization, the sick people whom Christ Jesus encountered
had forgotten 'the names of the Fathers in the heavens, the
names of the spirits of the higher hierarchies .... Now he (Christ

Jesus) knew that living in daily bread was what had sundered human beings from the heavens, and inevitably drove people into egotism and subjected them to the sway of Ahriman.'[37]

The people who subsequently became the followers of Christ Jesus and formed the first, still wide-ranging circle of his disciples, experienced his healing power within a world-historical context. Christ recognized that he must open up a path of return to the spirit for fallen, over-incarnated earthly human beings and their increasingly materializing culture, through new mysteries that no longer taught the incarnation secret of the human being but instead would make possible a reconnection with the cosmos, the divine, spiritual world:

> And then the earth experience of the God dawned in
> him: I must tell human beings not how the gods led the
> way from spirit down to earth but how human beings can
> find their way upward again from the earth to spirit.[38]

In this situation, said Steiner, Christ decided to renew the 'most ancient meditations and prayers', primarily that 'all-prevailing prayer' which he had heard years previously resounding from the sun sphere.

> He knew that human beings must now seek the path into
> worlds of spirit from below upwards, so that they could
> seek the divine spirit through this prayer. He therefore
> took the last lines of the old prayer, 'You Fathers in the
> heavens' and reversed it. This is the form appropriate for
> people of the modern era who now relate not to the many
> spiritual beings of the hierarchies, but to a single spirit
> being, Our Father, who art in heaven.
> He then reversed the penultimate line of this mystery
> prayer, And forgot your names to form the second line in
> the way necessary for people of the new era: Hallowed be
> thy name. In accordance with the feelings necessary if we

wish to approach the godhead by ascending from below, he transformed the third last line, Because man sundered himself from your kingdom into Thy kingdom come. Wherein the will of heaven does not rule, which human beings could no longer hear, he made into, Thy will be done on earth as it is in heaven for a complete reversal was necessary to find the path into worlds of spirit.

The secret of 'bread' – of incorporation in the physical body which had become fully apparent to him through Ahriman's goading, he transformed so that human beings would sense how this physical world also derives from the world of spirit, even though we may not directly perceive this. Thus the line became, Give us this day our daily bread. And the words, Trespass of selfhood through others incurred he reversed to make, Forgive us our trespasses, as we forgive them that trespass against us. And the second line in the old prayer of the mysteries, Witness to separating I-hood, he reversed by saying, but deliver us. Finally, he turned the first line, The evils hold sway, into from evil. Amen. And thus what Christianity received as the Lord's Prayer, the new mystery prayer taught by Christ, emerged through reversing what Jesus had once ... heard at the pagan altar.

According to Rudolf Steiner, this whole process was the background and underlying context for giving the microcosmic Lord's Prayer that arose by reversing its original macrocosmic form to the disciples, as later described by the evangelists Matthew and Luke. 'We could call it, "the reversed Lord's Prayer".'[39] Both prayers belong to the realm of the mysteries, ancient and new.

Rudolf Steiner never referred to the specific moment and circumstances in which the Lord's Prayer was given to the disciples. On one occasion he pointed to the fact that the Lord's Prayer was among the prayers 'given at the most solemn

moments of humanity's history'.[40] It marked a new beginning
in the evolution of the human I towards a spiritual community,
involving a new connection with the powers of the cosmos.
According to Steiner, in the 'mood of Christ-expectancy in
the ancient mysteries,' a yearning for this innovative impulse
had long existed.[41] And since the nineteenth century many
theologians have indicated that elements of the Lord's Prayer
are already present in the Old Testament (including the Jewish-
Aramaic Kaddish prayer).[42]

The appearance and activity of Christ Jesus, though, endowed
the long-prepared path with a radical new dimension, connected
with the human being's I, with his individuality: 'If we compare
these former versions of the phrases in the Lord's Prayer with the
Lord's Prayer itself, we discover that the Lord's Prayer sought
everywhere to lead what had once been spoken without invoking
the I to being spoken with invoking the I.'[43]

The 'kingdom' of the cosmic Christ being was to gain entry
into the human I (Thy kingdom come), and the cosmic will
of the Father was to be enacted on earth through the human
being (Thy will be done on earth as it is in heaven). The cosmic
spirit was to take inner hold of the I – Thy holy spirit descend
upon us and lead us through purification (catharsis) – while full
human I consciousness was maintained, and in fact enlarged and
intensified.

> The important thing is that Christ Jesus inaugurated
> a process of human evolution founded upon the I and
> its full preservation. He inaugurated and established I
> initiation. And thus we can say that this I is the core, the
> centre of the whole human entelechy; and that as it were
> all contemporary human nature is gathered into the I,
> and all that entered the world through the Christ event in
> pursuance of this I can also encompass all other parts and
> aspects of human nature.[44]

In calling the microcosmic Lord's Prayer the 'new mystery prayer', Rudolf Steiner was indirectly designating the new mysteries as those of the I in its cosmic connection with the 'Fathers in the heavens'.[45] 'Anthroposophy is a path of cognition that seeks to lead the spirit in the human being to the spirit in the universe', wrote Steiner nearly two thousand years after the time of Christ.[46] Thus he sought to realize the potential new mysteries facilitated by Christ's incarnation, and help them to gain ever more reality in human culture.

3. Having the Courage to Invoke the Name of The Father

The Lord's Prayer in Early Christianity

The Lord's Prayer lived in the community of disciples and original Christians, the congregations formed by the apostles. The sacred nature of the powerful words given by Christ, and his first speaking of the prayer to the Father, had an incisive effect on how the disciples related to it. Apart from Matthew and Luke, no early Christian texts reproduced the prayer's actual words; and the Gospel texts belonged to the inner circle of the early Christian community as esoteric treasure. According to Rudolf Steiner, the esoteric school of Paul knew the true meaning of the prayer.[1] In his epistles to the Romans (8:15) and to the Galatians (4:6), Paul was clearly referring indirectly to the Lord's Prayer in using the Aramaic word for Father (Abba). He also wrote to Timothy about deliverance from evil (2 Tim.4:18). However, he did not go any further than this in his exoteric texts in relation to the Lord's Prayer.

But at the beginning of the second century, the text of the Lord's Prayer was included in the Greek Didache, the Teaching of the Twelve Apostles, the oldest surviving catechism, aimed at the gentiles. The Didache gave instructions for liturgy and worship, and contained a collection of prayers including the Lord's Prayer. For the first time in the Didache, the doxology was added to the Lord's Prayer (in the Matthew version) in twofold form: For thine is the power and the glory, for ever. Unlike the original text, the prayer also ended with the Amen. The glorification of God, his doxa, at the end of the prayer, was borrowed from Old Testament forms (1Chr.29:10: 'Thine, O Lord, is the greatness, the power, the glory, the splendour and the majesty. For thine is all that is in heaven and upon earth.'[2]).

Althoff regarded the doxology as a possible indication that the Lord's Prayer was included in Christian worship from an early stage:

> Just as in Jewish worship the congregation responded to the reading of psalms by intoning a song of praise drawn from the same spiritual sphere as the psalm, so it is possible that the Lord's Prayer was spoken for the community by the priest and that the congregation responded to it with the solemnly spoken or sung doxology and Amen.

Althoff continues by saying that the doxology and the Amen were also evidence of inner development which the community of disciples and Christians underwent after the Lord's Prayer was given:

> The Whitsun event intervenes between the time when Christ gave the Lord's Prayer in ten lines in the Sermon on the Mount, and the time when the eleventh and twelfth lines of the prayer were added, completing it. It is as if the Lord's Prayer was given in ten lines (concluding with the plea for deliverance) so that it might be completed with two additional lines by those who passed through the Whitsun experience and thus achieved the maturity to augment it. They became capable of completing it out of the same higher inspiration that had first informed the whole configuration of the Lord's Prayer.[3]

We do not know precisely at what stage the Lord's Prayer was included in Christianity's rites and services. The worship of the original Christians took place on the day of the Resurrection, Sunday, on the Day of Christ, or 'Lord's Day' of which both the Revelation to John and the Didache speak. Prayers were directed towards the east, towards the rising sun in reference to the resurrected Christ whose second coming, or parousia, was expected from there. The Cross also hung on the east wall of the ritual space, evidence for which dates back to the second century.[4] The Aramaic Maranatha ('Come our Lord!') was passed down as the oldest liturgical prayer, and Paul makes reference to it in his First Letter to the Corinthians (16:22). In the Didache, the Maranatha prayer was mentioned in connection with the Last Supper. Oscar Cullmann, the Lutheran theologian, wrote:

> The fact that this prayer was passed on by Paul without translation in a letter composed in Greek, and that it retained this original form up to the time that the Didache was written, demonstrates the extraordinarily important role that this oldest prayer of the original Christian community must have had.[5]

On the evening of Maundy Thursday, the day before the Crucifixion, Christ established the Eucharist, the sacramental Last Supper ('Take, this is my body ... This is my blood.' Mark 14:22–24). On the evening of the Sunday of the Resurrection, three days later, Christ appeared to the disciples for the first time again, and stood in their midst 'as they sat at table' (Mark 16:14). Just a few hours previously two disciples in Emmaus had seen him, likewise when eating together, when blessing, breaking and sharing bread ('And their eyes were opened and they recognized him' Luke 24:31). Henceforth this presence of Christ was to continue in the Eucharist ('For where two or three are gathered together in my name, there am I in the midst of them.' Matt.18:20). At the same time, the inner stance of Christians was focused on his promised return, as the Maranatha ('Come our Lord!') suggested: in the Acts, we hear of the early

Christians that 'they devoted themselves to the apostles' teaching and fellowship, to the breaking of bread and the prayers' (Acts 2:42).

The Lord's Prayer is not found in the oldest versions of the Eucharist – either in the Apology of Justin Martyr (around AD 150) or in the Apostolic teachings of Hippolytus, whose text originated at the beginning of the third century. Not until the fourth century is there certain evidence of its inclusion in Christian worship, for example in the fifth Mystagogic Catechesis by Cyril of Jerusalem (c. AD 366).[6] Many reflections and writings are devoted to the question of whether Christ's words about 'praying in seclusion' may have shifted the Lord's Prayer (despite the fact of its emphasis on 'we') into the realm of the individual, who was to pray by withdrawing from the world (and thus also from the worshipping community) three times a day, as the Didache emphasized. All we know for sure is that the wording of the prayer, long kept secret and not committed to writing, was made available to those about to be baptized, who would therefore be accepted into the community of Christians.

> The text was only vouchsafed to those who belonged to the Church or were in the process of joining it, being initiated into its profundities during their preparation for baptism. Thus the oldest interpretations of the Lord's Prayer are catecheses addressed to candidates for baptism.[7]

In the liturgies of early Christianity, the Lord's Prayer does in fact first appear in relation to baptism. Together with the Creed, it formed part of the concluding teaching to the catechumens or candidates to whom Christ's teaching, the prayers, and acts of worship, were gradually revealed. Until they were baptized, the candidates were not privy to the Last Supper communion (missa fidelium) which was a rite enacted in strict privacy within the Christian community. During the last period of their preparation for baptism, the text of the Lord's Prayer was then divulged to them: they first heard it as part of the service of worship, during a Scrutiny Mass held by the bishop, and then began to live with it. Shortly before they were baptized, standing in a raised position in the church, they had to speak the Lord's Prayer aloud, and by heart, in the presence of the bishop. All this took place in the weeks and days preceding Easter. The baptism itself took place on the eve of Easter:

> When Easter eve, the time of baptism, arrived, the candidates for baptism received the sacrament and were then allowed to pray the Lord's Prayer for the first time. It was prayed standing, with the gaze directed upwards, the hands raised in the Orans gesture. Only now were the baptized ones truly 'children of the Father' in the full sense. Apostolic constitutions (at the end of the fourth century) express it as follows: 'When the baptized step forth from the font, they speak the Lord's Prayer for the first time.'

The sacrament of Confirmation followed directly after the sacrament of Baptism and the speaking of the Lord's Prayer:

> Anointing with holy oils followed directly after the Lord's Prayer had been spoken: the sacrament of Confirmation consolidated what the Lord had done for those who followed him, and impressed the seal of the name 'Christ' upon the forehead of the faithful – a name that henceforth they were to hold sacred and for the hallowing of which they had just prayed.[8]

After this, the bishop preached to these new members of the Christian community about the rite that had just been enacted, mostly doing so in the form of an interpretation of the Lord's Prayer.

In the fourth century, in texts relating to the liturgy for

the Mass, the Lord's Prayer was included as the prayer said immediately before Communion – as the Communion prayer of all liturgies of the Christian Church.[9] It was spoken after the Transubstantiation and the Intercession for the living and dead, and in some places (especially the Eastern Church) by the whole congregation, unlike the Eucharist prayer that was the sole responsibility of the priest.[10]★ In the Eastern Church a preparatory prayer was added to the Lord's Prayer – the petition to pray to God with a pure heart and to be allowed to refer to him as Father. In the St James liturgy, first transcribed in Jerusalem at the end of the fourth century, the Lord's Prayer is preceded by these words: 'Make us worthy, good Lord, so that we may call upon you courageously and uncondemned, with purity of heart and illumined soul, without shame and with holy lips: you, the holy God, the Father in heaven.'[11]

In the Byzantine Mass, these words were spoken: 'And make us worthy, Lord, that with trust, without reproach, we may dare to invoke you, the God of heaven, as Father, and to say: Our Father, who art in the heaven.'[12]

In the East Syrian liturgy (the Apostles' Anaphora), the preparatory prayer runs:

> May your peace, Lord, dwell amongst us, and your peace in our hearts, and may our tongue proclaim your truth, your Cross be the guardian of our souls, as we make our mouth into new harps and speak a new language with fiery lips. Make us worthy, Lord, with the trust that comes from you, to speak before you this pure and holy prayer that your life-giving mouth taught your faithful disciples, the children of your mysteries: When you pray, you should pray and avow thus, saying: Our Father, who art in heaven ...[13]

Speaking the Lord's Prayer as part of the act of worship and maintaining an awareness of, and reverence for, the distinctive nature of the prayer of Christ's disciples, remained as great as ever. Likewise a preparatory prayer preceded every reading of Gospel texts during worship, petitioning for purity of heart and lips; but the Lord's Prayer belonged already in the communion sphere which it immediately preceded.[14] In an Old Spanish Mozarabic Mass (of Christians living under Arab rule), the congregation responded to the fourth petition of the Lord's Prayer with, 'Quia tu Deus est' ('For you, O Lord, is this bread').[15] The position of the Lord's Prayer between the transformation of substance and the act of communion unmistakeably took the realm of the bread into the mystery of the body of Christ.

The first exegeses of the Lord's Prayer for catechumens (candidates being instructed) in the third century had accentuated this Christological dimension of the 'daily bread', as Cyprian's words (echoed by Tertullian and Origen) clearly show: 'We ask each day that this bread, that is Christ be given unto us.'[16] Since then it has been asked whether the Lord's Prayer might not have been part of the Lord's Supper liturgy from the beginning, even if it was not referred to in written records before the fourth century.[17] At any event, it was considered to be an inner preparation for the encounter with Christ's body and blood, and a petition for forgiveness of sins. Augustine spoke of the Lord's Prayer being for him like a 'washing of the face' before approaching the altar.[18] It is possible that in the first centuries it was prayed quietly by every Christian during worship, before communion.

Tertullian wrote his treatise on prayer (De oratione) around the year 200. It contains the oldest surviving Lord's Prayer exegesis in Christendom. Tertullian, who came from Carthage in North Africa, wrote his text in Rome where he lived from 190. He subscribed to Platonic philosophy (and to that of the Stoics) and De oratione was addressed to candidates for baptism, based on the Lord's Prayer as the concentration of all Christ's teachings and as the basis for all prayer. Like the Didache, and drawing on an Old Testament passage (Dan.6:10), he recommended praying the Lord's Prayer three times a day, at the third, sixth and ninth hour. Clearly this was intended to establish and ritualize a spiritual process that Christ Jesus, two centuries before, had expressly placed in individual freedom.

Tertullian understood the Lord's Prayer as a prayer for each individual. In the petition Our Father, who art in the heaven he left out the noster ('our') (Pater qui in caelis es) despite otherwise following the text of Matthew's Gospel.[19] The whole process of which the prayer speaks was to take place 'in us', in the human I. God was to be hallowed 'within us', according to Tertullian, and within us too, in the human I, his will should be done and his kingdom come. This dimension of Christ in the I was one Tertullian also connected with the petition for bread: 'We should regard this expression, "daily bread" in largely spiritual terms.' Christ is the mystic and sacramental bread. The candidates for baptism, whose instruction Tertullian had in mind, stood at the threshold of the sacramental Lord's Supper community of Christ: 'Through asking for our daily bread, we pray to be permitted to live in unbroken community with Christ, and not to be sundered from his body.' Even if, in the time of Tertullian, the Lord's Prayer was not yet part of the official liturgy of the Mass, it occupied a key position in baptism as the approach to the Eucharist and the 'gateway' to all sacraments (as Aquinas wrote eight hundred years later).[20] In this sense, 'bread' had a Christological dimension for Tertullian: it belonged to human existence in the sense of daily need, but also to the dimension of the I (and Christ-I). Rittelmeyer wrote:

On four occasions, bread appears at a significant place in the life of Christ: in the temptation he relinquishes it. In the Lord's Prayer he petitions for it. In the feeding of the five thousand he dispenses it. At the Last Supper he transforms it. That is the history of bread in the life of Christ. That is the history of bread upon the earth. Over it, though, shines the phrase: 'I am the bread of life.' In the story of the temptation, Christ says: 'Man lives not by bread alone but from each Word that issues from the mouth of God.' This Word lives on in the life of Christ and develops into the saying: 'My food is this, that I do the will of him who sent me, and fulfil his work.' And the final culmination is the phrase: 'I am the bread of life.'[21]

In his Esoteric Lord's Prayer, Rudolf Steiner wrote the lines:

In overflowing abundance you give us
spiritual nourishment, the bread of life,
through all changing conditions
of our lives.

★

The study of the Lord's Prayer by Origen followed just three decades after that of Tertullian. Origen's teacher, Clement of Alexandria, had written about prayer in the eighth book of his Stromata. Rudolf Steiner spoke as follows about the early Church Fathers:

If you would really take the trouble to study how
someone like Clement the Alexandrian, his pupil Origen,
even Tertullian or Irenaeus, not to mention older
teachers of the Church, drew very largely on the pagan
initiation principle as their point of departure and then
found their way through to Christianity in their own
manner – if you study minds such as these you will find
that a very distinctive kind of inner mobility lived in their
concepts and ideas. A quite different spirit lived in these
figures than later in humanity's history. The spirit that
lived in them is one we need to find an affinity with if we
ourselves wish to approach the Mystery of Golgotha. The

important thing here is to find our way into this spirit and outlook![22]

In his Stromata, Clement had argued that a person's whole life should be a prayer, a life lived in God's presence: 'All his comments on prayer are founded on the presiding idea that prayer composes a true Christian's whole life, and therefore involves uninterrupted, intimate communication with God.'[23] He saw prayer as the 'state of openness to God', as reverent contemplation of the divine spirit, in the sense both of the Greek mysteries and their (later) philosophy of religion, but also of the Gospel of John. This prayerful stance distinguishes the person who lives contemplatively with thoughts turned to God and is embodied in the single act of prayer with raised hands and eyes turned towards heaven. After Clement's pupil Origen was expelled from Alexandria and founded a new school in Caesarea (Palestine), he wrote comprehensively about the nature of the Lord's Prayer in a study written in 233/34 called Peri Euches (On Prayer). Tertullian, and after him Cyprian, also wrote for baptismal candidates.

The Lord's Prayer, according to Origen, is prayed with the Holy Spirit. It does not just petition this spirit but, as the Gospel of Luke tells us ('Thy Holy Spirit come upon us and cleanse us'), is enacted with its help.[24] 'Our spirit is unable to pray alone if the Holy Spirit does not also pray for us and as it were before us as listener.'[25] Origen says that the angels, along with fellow Christians who have died, join us as we pray the Lord's Prayer. He wrote as follows about the efficacy and importance of the angels for prayer:

> This is illumined for us by the fact that Raphael brings
> before God a prayer offering from Tobit and Sarah.
> For after both had prayed, the Holy Script says, 'The
> prayer of both was heard in the presence of the glory of
> the great God. And Raphael was sent to heal the two of

them' (Tobit 3:16f). And as Raphael himself reveals the
service he has done them as angel, by the direction of
God, he says, 'So now God sent me to heal you and your
daughter-in-law Sarah. I am Raphael, one of the seven
holy angels who present the prayers of the saints and
enter into the presence of the glory of the Holy One.'
(Tobit 12:14f).[26]

In another text, Origen states: 'When people of firm resolve,
taking the better as their goal, pray to God, then thousands of
holy powers join unasked in prayer with them.'[27]

Like his teacher Clement, whose school in Alexandria he
had attended in his youth, Origen wrote in reference to Paul,
(1Thess.5:17) of 'uninterrupted prayer' and described the 'saint's
life' as 'one long prayer'.[28] According to Origen, awareness of
Our Father, who art in the heavens permeates the life of the
pious, God-surrendering, holy, person. Along with John and
Paul, Origen too spoke of receiving the spirit of 'Sonship', thus
becoming the child of God: 'But to all who received him, who
believed in his name, he gave power to become children of God
(John 1:12). This, says Origen, gives rise to the mission for us
to become 'true sons', so that we may rightfully speak the word
'Father' (Abba).[29] The locus of our encounter with God, he says,
lies exclusively in the human I, the Hegemonikon, the seat of our
divine likeness.[30] There too the 'kingdom of God' is established
as blissful state, founded by human beings who bear the 'image of
the heavenly' (1Cor.15:49) within themselves and have therefore
become 'heavenly ones'.[31] According to Origen – and as Paul
wrote to Philemon (3:14) – we need to 'press on toward the goal'
or reach out to what stands before us, and in words and deeds
form and broaden the kingdom of Christ. Rudolf Steiner said,
'May your kingdom grow more expansive in our deeds and in
the conduct of our lives.'

Like Tertullian, Origen also saw the petition for bread as
participation in the being of Christ. He did not speak of 'daily'

but of 'immanent' bread (corresponding to the ousia, the human being's spiritual nature), deriving this in philological terms from the unusual word epousios in the Greek text of the Lord's Prayer.[32]* Origen, who suffered a great deal in his life and died as a martyr, also addressed the implications of the two last petitions relating to temptation and evil. He stressed that the aim of the Lord's Prayer was not to nullify temptation but – as with Job – to acknowledge that 'all human life on earth is a temptation' (Job 7:1 Vulgate). He emphasized the meaning of temptation as a trial whereby one could become good: God, he said, used the existence of evil as a test and probation.

Before Origen, Paul also spoke of the impossibility of freedom from temptation, writing to the first Christians of Corinth that God would not tempt them beyond their capacity but would shape the outcome in such a way that 'you may be able to endure it' (1Cor.10:13).[33] In this vein, Origen also stressed that God allows no temptation of us that is beyond our (potential) capacity to cope with. The human being, however, is never free from temptation, and as a Christian will be engaged in continuing spiritual battle 'with the powers and potencies and dominions of this darkness and the spirit beings of evil.'[34] Paul had written to the Ephesians: 'For we are not contending against flesh and blood, but against the principalities, against the powers, against the world rulers of this present darkness, against the spiritual hosts of wickedness in the heavenly places' (Eph.6:12). In view of this basic spiritual context and the existential situation for Christians, Origen states that we must prepare ourselves now for future battles – in other words, should arm ourselves against the adversaries and the temptations they initiate, so that we are not delivered up to them 'unprepared'. Thus, with Paul, we are 'hard pressed on all sides but not vanquished' and ask our Father that we may not succumb.[35]

A millennium after Origen, Thomas Aquinas (like Augustine before him) wrote similarly of the sixth petition of the Lord's Prayer. He cited the Epistle of James (1:13), 'Let no one say

when he is tempted, "I am tempted by God"; for God cannot be
tempted with evil and he himself tempts no one,' and emphasised
like Origen, 'You must know that Christ does not teach us to
pray so that we are not tempted but so that we do not succumb
to temptation.'[36] 'Blessed is the man who endures trial, for when
he has stood the test he will receive the crown of life which God
has promised to those who love him' (Jas.1:12). Rudolf Steiner
formulated the Apostles' Lord's Prayer, as follows:

> You do not allow the tempter to work in us beyond the
> capacity of our strength – for no temptation can prevail
> in your being; and the tempter is only appearance and
> delusion, from which you will safely deliver us, Father,
> through the light of your knowledge.

According to Origen, we have to confront and prevail over
evil: 'God does not deliver us ... from evil when his enemy fails
to confront us in battle with his wiles and manifold weapons and
the agents of his will, but rather when we are bravely steadfast
and stand firm to win victory.'[37]

On the evening of Maundy Thursday in the High Priestly
Prayer, Christ spoke these words to his Father: 'I do not pray that
thou shouldst take them out of the world, but that thou shouldst
keep them from the evil one' (John 17:15). The light of the
first three petitions of the Lord's Prayer is to prevail within the
darkness of the earthly sphere and gradually transform it through
'consecration in truth', that is, through human development to
higher levels. 'Within you rages the battle that must be fought ...
the enemy comes forth out of your own heart.'[38]

★

The third century works by Tertullian and Origen and also
Cyprian's text De Dominica oratione, originating around 250,
disseminated early Christianity's understanding of the Lord's

Prayer. Increasingly, translations of the Lord's Prayer were also made in other languages.[39] The most influential of all was the work of Jerome undertaken at the end of the fourth century, at the instigation of Pope Damasus. He translated the whole Bible into Latin, leaving largely unaltered an old translation of the Lord's Prayer from the first century.[40] 'There is huge significance in the fact ... that the substance of Christianity spreads in this way through following centuries, and that the Latin language serves this dissemination from the fourth century.'[41]

Just two decades before Jerome, the missionary Wulfila, whose mother was a Greek from Cappadocia, had completed his very different translation, creating a Gothic Bible. Althoff wrote of this work:

> To do this he [Wulfila] had to transform a language that
> hitherto had lived only in oral form, in mythic images
> and epic songs, into a written language that was capable
> of giving the Goths an inward experience of the lofty
> content of the message of Christ. In a most brilliant way
> he coined new words from Germanic word-stems and
> root syllables. This transformed language became a vessel
> in which high poetic power of expression was married to
> profound inwardness. This enabled the Goths to engage
> fully with the message of light, life and love. That Wulfila
> succeeded in doing this is one of the greatest cultural
> achievements. It can be shown that the Gothic language
> made headway amongst the young Germanic tribes of
> Central Europe as the medium of worship and culture,
> conveying an understanding of Christ that developed
> quite independently of official ecclesiastical institutions,
> and before St Boniface arrived amongst the Germans.
> Borne on this language, a new awareness dawned in
> lands north of boundaries marked by the spread of the
> olive tree. The 'catastrophe of the gods' which young
> Germanic tribes experienced in historically tangible

ways and which initially left them 'god-bereft' led them to take up the mystery of the Christus in unsis (Christ in us) as that of the innuma frauja (inner ruler). Thus they developed a new sense of I in the depths of their souls and sensibilities, one realized in triggwa (loyalty, faithfulness). In this way the New Testament became for them the niujo triggwa (the new faithfulness).[42]

Wulfila's translation of the Lord's Prayer runs as follows:

Atta unsar thu in himinam,
Weihnai namo thein.
Qimai thiudinassus theins.
Wairthai wilja theins, swe in himina jah ana airthai.
Hlaif unsarana thana sinteinan gif uns himma daga.
Jah aflet uns thatei skulans sijaima, swaswe jah weis
afletam thaim skulam unsaraim.
Jah ni briggais uns in fraistubnjai,
ak lausei uns af thamma ubilin;
Unte theina ist thiudangardi jah mahts jah wutlhus
in aiwins. Amen.[43]

In his lecture in Dornach on May 15, 1921, Rudolf Steiner read aloud the whole Gothic version of the Lord's Prayer from his notebook, then commented:

If we grasp this prayer, that is so wonderful in Wulfila's language, and try to translate it into our own [German] language, we must not translate literally but instead render it roughly like this:

We feel you above in the spiritual heights
All-father of men.
Hallowed be thy name.
May thy realm of dominion come to us.

May thy will hold sway, as in the heavens
so also on the earth.

And we have to really feel what is expressed here. The
person who translated the Lord's Prayer in this way
felt something primordial. Basically he felt as all these
pagans felt: that in spiritual heights lives the all-sustaining
Father of humanity, whom they pictured through ancient
clairvoyance as the king, the invisible, supersensible
king holding sway like no earthly king. They addressed
him as the king amongst the free Goths, expressing this
by saying: Atta unsar thu in himinam. And then they
addressed his threefold being: Hallowed be thy name.
They saw this name – you can compare this with the
ancient Sanskrit meanings – as the being who comes to
expression, who reveals himself outwardly in the same
way that the human being reveals himself in his body.
By the 'realm of dominion' they understood the power
that was able, as it were, to hold sway over their realm.
Weihnai namo thein Qimai thiudinassus theins. Wairthai
wilja theins, swe in himina jah ana airthai.

By 'will' they understood the spirit that shone through
the power and the name. And thus they gazed upwards
and in the spirit of supersensible worlds saw a threefold
spirituality holding sway there. It was this to which they
raised themselves, saying: Jah ana airthai. Hlaif unsarana
thana sinteinan gif uns himma daga. Let it be so equally
on the earth through thy name, as that through which
you reveal yourself and which is to be hallowed, so that
which reveals itself in us externally, and must be daily
renewed, be so illumined likewise.

We just have to grasp what lies in the old Gothic word
Hlaif (body; in German, Leib). This is the root of Laib,
loaf of bread. When we say today 'Give us this day our
daily bread', people no longer have a sense of what this

originally conveyed. By contrast the word Hlaif here means: As we hold thy name to be the body, so let our body become alike, through its nourishment, through what it absorbs in metabolism.

In the same way that a transition is then made to the realm of dominion or rulership that is to hold sway in supersensible worlds, so a transition is made to what holds sway in the social order between human beings. There, people encounter each other without one being in the other's debt. Amongst the Goths this word skulan, 'debt', really does mean owing something to the other in a social context, both in a moral and physical (or pecuniary) sense.

Thus in the same way that a transition was made from the name to the realm of dominion, and so from bodily nature to the spirit (for in supersensible terms the 'name' means roughly the same as corporeal nature), a transition was made from the soul to the realm of dominion. So likewise a connection was made between the external body and the interpersonal soul realm, and then to what is intrinsically spiritual: 'Let us not lapse or succumb.' Jah aflet uns thatei skulans sijaima, swaswe jah weis afletan thaim skulam unsaraim, which means: 'Let us not succumb to what arises from our body to occlude our spirit, but deliver us from the evils that plunge our spirit in darkness.' Jah ni briggais uns in fraistubnjai ak lausei uns af thamma ubilin, 'Deliver us from the evils,' which could arise however, if the spirit fell too deeply into the nature of the body.

The second part of the prayer, therefore, roughly expresses the following: social existence on earth should be ordered as above in the spiritual heights of heaven. This is reinforced by saying that we wish to acknowledge such a spiritual order here on earth. Unte theina ist thiudangardi jah maths jah wulthus in aiwins. Amen.

All-father, whose name forms the external embodiment
of the spirit, whose realm of dominion we wish to
acknowledge, and whose will should hold sway, you,
you should also penetrate the earthly realm so that we
daily see our body arise anew, as it were through earthly
nourishment. So that we do not become the debtors
of each other in social existence, so that we meet one
another as equals, so that our spiritual-bodily nature
does not succumb or fall, so that we connect the trinity
of earthly social existence with the supersensible; for the
supersensible should hold sway, should be emperor and
king. The supersensible should hold sway on earth rather
than the life of the senses, the personal life.

Unte theina ist thiudangardi jah maths jah wulthus in
aiwins. Amen.

For thine is the claim to dominion rather than any
thing or being here on earth, and thine is the right to
power, thine is the revelation of light, of glory, of all-
prevailing social love.

This gives expression to the supersensible Trinity
that should penetrate the sensory social order on
earth. And once again this is re-affirmed at the end by
acknowledging that, yes, we wish to order social existence
in this way, in a threefold way as above in the heavens:
for thine is the kingdom, thine is the power, thine is the
revelation. Theina ist thiudangardi jah maths jah wulthus
in aiwins. Amen.[44]

★

Rudolf Steiner was hugely impressed with Wulfila's life's
work. It belonged to the roots of European Christianity, and
was exemplary as a 'founding archetype' of the spirit of social
life.[45] It was imbued with the initiation elements of an ancient
clairvoyance that still lived in many countries and cultures in

the centuries following the event of Golgotha. On July 16, 1922, Steiner said in Dornach:

> The event of Golgotha occurred at a time when a great deal of ancient initiation wisdom, ancient initiation knowledge, still existed. And it is true to say that sufficient numbers of people employed ancient initiation wisdom to understand the Golgotha event by means of supersensible insight. Initiates sought to employ all that they could gather in the shape of initiation knowledge in order to understand how a being like the Christ, who was not united with earthly evolution prior to the time of the Mystery of Golgotha, connected with an earthly body and now remains united with human evolution. What kind of being this is, and what it underwent before descending into the earthly realm – all such questions were answered only by turning to the highest initiation faculties at the time of Golgotha. But now we see that ancient initiation wisdom – which certainly existed in the Near and Middle East, in North Africa, and also within Hellenic culture, even extending to Italy and even further West into Europe – met with ever less understanding from the fifth century ad.[46]

Steiner repeatedly highlighted the radical changes in western countries that occurred in the fourth century, and brought with them a consolidation of the Roman Catholic power structure and the end of original Christianity.[47] Thus ended a period when the esoteric content of Hellenism, of the Gnosis and of northern European initiation had permeated Christianity, and when the teachings of the resurrected Christ were still full of vitality.[48]★ The pagan, spiritual insight into the Gospels of someone like Wulfila were gradually suppressed by Roman Catholic elements and, according to Steiner, their increasingly externalized and 'dead' rites.[49] 'You see, in Europe Christianity really did gradually pass over into world dominion.'[50]

From the fourth century onwards, the Lord's Prayer became part of the Church's official liturgy of the Mass and much of the spirit of both the individual and social intimacy of its Christ-dimension and mystery context was lost. It is possible also that diminution of its vitality was what finally allowed the prayer of Christ's disciples, long kept shrouded in secrecy, to be adopted by the prevailing order, and to be fixed in symbolic, externalized and increasingly abstract rites which – according to Steiner – increasingly replaced an experience of 'the living communion' of the Lord's Supper. What arose and grew to be ever more dominant was the Church as outer institution, whose Latin rites were not understood by the majority of people and which worked 'suggestively' and were intended to do so.[51] The ensouled spirituality living in Wulfila's translation and connected with his people and time, and thus also with old religious rites and content, receded – as Rudolf Steiner described in striking terms in his Whitsun 1921 lectures in Dornach.[52]

4. A Dialogue with the Divine
The Inner Space of a 'Thought Mantra'

Never before or since has so much been said with so few words. As if laden with heavenly powers we return from these petitions to the earth. The word-body of the Lord's Prayer is as concentrated as possible, but the spirit that indwells it encompasses heaven and earth. And the Lord's Prayer also, and in particular, directs us to 'hidden realms'. It is like entering the inner nature of God when, in the first three petitions, we are led from the name to the kingdom, and from the kingdom into the will. And it is an entry, too, into the inner nature of the human being when, in the last four petitions, we are led from need to sin, from sin to temptation, and from temptation to the power of evil.

Friedrich Rittelmeyer[1]

At the beginning of the twentieth century, in his Apostles' Lord's Prayer, Rudolf Steiner created a German version of the Lord's Prayer that breathes the spirit of early Christianity and patrology, the movement of the early Christian centuries that arose in the context of Greek culture and, especially, Platonism. The distinctive view of the meaning of 'name', 'kingdom' and 'will', as also of 'bread', 'debt' and 'evil' that existed and developed amongst Clement, Origen and others, found its way into Steiner's new version as can be demonstrated by close study.

Steiner's esoteric exegesis of the Lord's Prayer in January 1907 took (at least apparently) a different point of departure. His lectures in Berlin, Karlsruhe and Cologne related to anthroposophical mystery knowledge. He did not speak of patrology but aimed to show that the Lord's Prayer corresponds to the human being's evolutionary spiritual-physical constitution. The ancient mysteries, said Steiner in his lectures on the Fifth Gospel, were aware of the conditions and the tragedy of human incarnation. Here he explored in meditative fashion how the development of self-awareness came at the price of loss of cosmic vision. At the time of Christ, and following his embodiment and activity, a radical change was introduced which became apparent not least in a reversal of the old mystery prayers. The human being's reconnection with the cosmos out of the awoken powers of his I, his innermost being, became an evolutionary momentum for the future.

Rudolf Steiner repeatedly showed that true understanding of this mystery dimension of the Christ event lived only in the esoteric school of Paul – a school whose leadership Paul entrusted to his 'most intimate pupil', Dionysius the Areopagite, while he himself had to represent Christianity exoterically in the world.[2]★ Steiner's hermetic study of the Lord's Prayer in 1907 was given in accordance with the spirit of the esoteric school of Paul, which continued the tradition of pre-Christian mystery schools yet also signified something fundamentally new and innovative. 'Within this esoteric school of Christianity, the inner circle of pupils received the secret doctrine which you too are now learning of through science of the spirit,' said Steiner on March 17, 1907 in Munich.[3]

In the context of anthroposophical or hermetic insight into the human being that was long kept within closed circles (in Rosicrucian communities amongst others), Rudolf Steiner spoke of the seven petitions of the Lord's Prayer that address the diverse levels of the human entelechy. The early Christian fathers, too, had repeatedly drawn attention to the threefold and fourfold structure in the Lord's Prayer: 'Three petitions are directed to the heavenly realm and four to this life,' wrote Jerome in the fourth century.[4] But in Steiner's account this sevenfold form is based on the human being's seven aspects or levels of being, each of which reveals a distinct evolutionary situation addressed by the Lord's Prayer as a new mystery prayer.

★

Steiner says that the upper triad of the seven petitions relates to the 'higher core of the human being', the 'germinal disposition for higher development which in fact issues from the highest spiritual entity: the threefold, higher human being, the divine core of being, our divine potential.'[5] 'Spirit man', 'life spirit' and 'spirit self' are, according to Steiner, not only the three highest principles of human nature and thus the goal of spiritual development, but also three principles in the godhead itself.[6] With our upper triad, which is only germinally present in us but already lives in and around us in incipient form, we reach up into the heavenly sphere. The first petitions of the Lord's Prayer are drawn from this higher spiritual human nature – they address the divine spirit, and at the same time also our inmost future potential, our true developmental goal. As invocations of the divine they are at the same time a 'self-summoning'[7]

> Our Father, who art in heaven – this points to the deepest soul ground of human nature, to the inmost human entelechy that, in accord with Christian esotericism, belongs to the realm of spirit ...
>
> Once [human beings] have developed this most profound, most inward nature, then they have transformed their being through gradual development into what is called the 'Father' in Christianity. What rests concealed in the human soul and hovers before us as the great goal of humanity, is the Father in heaven ... We have to reach out, striving, through the three higher aspects to the Father in heaven, through the name, kingdom and will.[8]

In his Esoteric Lord's Prayer, Rudolf Steiner formulated this view of the beginning of the prayer as follows:

Father, you who were, are, and will be
in the inmost being of all of us!

This Esoteric Lord's Prayer did not start with the first petition, Hallowed be thy name, but with the third, Thy will be done. The universe originally first arose out of the will of the godhead, the creative will within divine being and the capacity of sacrifice.[9] The godhead made development possible out of powers that are the substantial foundation of all existence. Steiner tells us that an image of this creative power of will lives in us, if only in germinal form. But by the end of planetary evolution we will have developed the level of our being that Steiner called 'spirit man' (or atma) and described as having the 'quality of will' ('the basic character of this highest divine principle in us is a kind of will'): 'The inner nature of what has so far developed in us only to the weakest degree is will; and in future, as we increasingly rise higher in our development, this is to become our most splendid attribute and principle.'[10]

Steiner spoke of the pure, most highly developed level of will, that which serves development, undertakes tasks with devotion and allows something new to arise through self-sacrifice. Understood in this way, the will is the Father God principle within the Trinity and underpins all existence. But as human beings we are called upon to lead the earth's evolution forward, as the future tenth hierarchy of love and freedom.[11] Now and in future our capacity and mission is to collaborate creatively in the world's unfolding development, and to develop a pure will that then becomes our 'most splendid principle'. In lectures in 1920 and 1921, two seven-year periods after his first lectures on the Lord's Prayer, Steiner said,

In the period of earthly evolution that follows the
Mystery of Golgotha, the human aspect that must

especially be developed is that of the will. In relation
to their will, people of olden times lived in a very dim
awareness. But the will must be imbued with wisdom,
with the power of ideas, with spirituality. This is the
important thing. It is therefore of primary importance
for the Christ impulse to gain entry into the human will.
We just have to understand this in the right way. Now
and moving into the future, development of the will is of
very special importance. In relation to the will we have to
become ever more conscious and aware.[12]

The will is in future destined to become something
very mighty, cosmic: to become something by means
of which we will in future belong to and be part of the
whole cosmos. Though an individual being, we will
nevertheless enact our individual impulses as cosmic
reality.[13]

May we enact your will in our life as you, Father, have
enshrined it in our inmost heart and soul.

The creative divine will, with its capacity to sacrifice itself,
allowed the earth to arise with all its beings. It gave rise to the
kingdom as a reflection of the godhead. Rudolf Steiner illustrated
this on January 28, 1907 in Berlin with the image of the sun
emerging from a central point, the centre of creative will, the
spherical periphery coming into existence as he did many years later
in a school lesson in Stuttgart (p. 25). 'Thus the will is the central
point – the kingdom is a reflection of the will.'[14] Creation, the
kingdoms of nature, live out of the sacrificing spirit of the godhead
to which they owe their life and existence. In the kingdom, an
active, creating principle is at work – the Christ aspect of the
Trinity whose microcosmic reflection can arise in us as 'life spirit'
(buddhi) in relation to the Christ being.[15] Thy kingdom come.

Finally Rudolf Steiner spoke of the names and the 'spirit self'
of the human being:

> The godhead appears in the kingdom in endless levels
> of being and in infinite multiplicity; and standing at
> this high level insofar as we can regard them as issuing
> from the divine, we distinguish these diverse beings and
> entities (as esoteric science does) by giving them their
> name. The name is what we then think of as the separate
> entity, and by means of which the separate parts of this
> great multiplicity are distinguished from one another. It
> is the third of the three highest human principles, and
> would correspond to manas or spirit self.[16]

The 'name' of what exists is existence raised up into consciousness, perceived or acknowledged being, and is related to the Spirit aspect of the Trinity. The hallowed name is the truth of particular existence, the consecration of the name. Althoff called it a 'carrying back of each thing to its origin, into the spirit light of the breadths of the cosmos in which its being originates.'[17] A person who develops the spirit self level of his own being becomes able to rediscover the true name of things of the kingdom, that is, the spiritual configuration of their existence, their place in the cosmos. (As Althoff said in the same place, 'Name is active energy, the power of configuration.'). The new mystery knowledge of the human being arises, says Steiner, from this quality of spirit self when a person grasps their own name and finds the names of the others, in an act of cognition that is a microcosmic reflection of the Holy Spirit. Rudolf Steiner once called anthroposophy the search for the 'lost Word'.[18] In the rediscovery of this Creation-Word lies the future of humanity.[19] Steiner said that the pupils of the esoteric school of early Christianity were told:

> Look at the things around you, whose manifold diversity
> is an expression of the godhead! If you say their names,
> you grasp them as parts of the divine world order.
> Whatever may be present in your surroundings, regard it

as sacred; and in the name you give to it, see something that makes it into a part of divine being. Hold it sacred, grow into the kingdom that issues from the godhead, and develop yourself upward to the will that will be an atma, but at the same time a part of the godhead.

...

If you wish to find yourselves in what you should ultimately raise yourself into, you will find that it is of the nature of will. If you wish to raise yourselves to the bearer of this will, of this atma, to buddhi, you will find that it constitutes the kingdom in the divine realm. And if you wish to raise yourselves to what you perceive as names, concepts or ideas of things, you will find it as manas in the divine realm.[20]

Thus Rudolf Steiner outlined the teachings of the esoteric school of Christianity in relation to the first three petitions of the Lord's Prayer, in highly condensed intimations of macrocosmic-microcosmic relationships. Subsequently he further elaborated this in his accounts of cosmology, both in lectures and books, and not least in his great work on the evolution of the earth, Esoteric Science. 'Anthroposophy,' he wrote in relation to the new Christian mysteries, 'is a path of cognition that seeks to lead the spirit in the human being to the spirit in the universe.'

★

'And the pupil was told: "You should be clear, even when you take a bite of bread, that this too is a thing in which the godhead dwells, and that it should therefore be sacred to you".'[21] The fourth petition of the Lord's Prayer, with which the second, earth-focused half of the prayer begins, is aimed at the level of physical life, says Steiner. Thomas Aquinas integrated into his exegesis of the Lord's Prayer the spiritual-Christological dimension of the 'bread' as Tertullian, Origen and Cyprian regarded it, but at the same time he also highlighted the aspect of physical preservation of life, quoting the Old Testament 'The essentials for life are water and bread' (Ecclus.29:21) and 'Remove far from me falsehood and lying; give me neither poverty nor riches; feed me with the food that is needful for me' (Prov.30:8).[22] Rudolf Steiner spoke of the level of the human physical body and its existence in transmutation of earthly substances:

> It [the physical body] is composed of the same substances and forces as the apparently lifeless world around us. The physical body could not survive if substance and strength did not continually flow into it from the surrounding physical world, continually and repeatedly rebuilding it anew. Really the physical body is a permanent transit station for everything it contains. In and out of it flow substances that also constitute the outer universe, and for a while we contain them ... We continually renew the substance of our physical body. What was once within us is now somewhere quite different, spread out in nature, while other substances have entered us. Bodily life is predicated on a continuous influx and departure of substance.[23]

Give us this day our daily bread.

The physical body is a part of the earth and thus also of the cosmos ('Its substance is taken from the substance of our planet and returns to it again').[24] When discussing the Lord's Prayer, Rudolf Steiner did not speak of the physical body's further evolution, but of its preservation. The four lower aspects of the human being – the physical body, etheric body, astral body and I organization – are not, unlike the upper triad, the active future principle. Rather the lower four live from the future evolution of the upper three, and are at permanent risk of degeneration, decline and corruption – of actual illness. The esoteric pupil was taught that the piece of bread he ate should be seen as sacred, and his understanding arises from the name of the upper triad; and in this sense a viable attitude towards nutritional substance becomes possible, combatting the danger of misuse and immoderation, in both surfeit and asceticism.

And forgive us our debts as we forgive our debtors. In the terminology of Christian esotericism, according to Steiner, debt (or trespass) is a lapse or error in the sphere of the human life body. This body – as bearer of memory but also of enduring personal qualities and habits, and thus of character – is one that, through the process of incarnation, we have in common with the human circumstances into which we were born.[25]

> Precisely the qualities which we have within us as permanent, unchanging ones, will be found not only in us but in everything to which we belong in any way – thus in our family, nation and so on. We can recognize individual members of a nation by their common habits and temperaments. So if we consider the life we share with the community into which we were born, we find that the characteristics arising from the fact that we belong to a family and nation, and which give us a sense of being related to this nation, also resemble the characteristics that live in our particular era. Human beings can develop mutual understanding through the shared qualities in their etheric bodies.[26]

The ether or life body, says Steiner, keeps balance with the other members of a community, in the sense of social obligations that include undertaking work for others.[27] The life body helps sustain the community to which we belong up to a certain point. A shortfall in this contribution to the community, a disturbance of balance in our relationship to it is, according to Rudolf Steiner, the esoteric Christian meaning of the word 'debt'. The petition for forgiveness of debts therefore implies concern with the healthy state of the etheric body. A lapse or weakening of this aspect thus not only impairs our relationship with the community but also with the spirituality of the cosmos, in which the individualized etheric body originates. Steiner tells us that this is cosmically determined in a fundamental way, and when life on earth is over our etheric substance returns to the cosmos.[28] The petition for preservation of the etheric body therefore also relates to the future of the human being amidst Creation, in the cosmos. It is true to say of the etheric body (as of the other three aspects of the lower four) that it will be preserved insofar as human spiritual development is properly accomplished in accord with the upper three.

And lead us not into temptation but deliver us from evil. Just as debt is connected with the configuration of the etheric body's forces, so temptation and evil are connected with the human soul body and I. The fall into temptation, states Steiner, is from an esoteric perspective a 'personal sin of the individual'; it is 'what can affect the astral body insofar as it is individually flawed'.[29] To distinguish between debt and sin, Steiner said on January 28, 1907 in Berlin:

> When a person commits errors through his ether or life body, he can become more of a sinner (debtor) in the circle of his fellows, failing more in his social obligations and their mutual interplay between people, which is what makes human society possible. But the sins which are more individual, through which a person is flawed only as distinct personality, are the lapses brought about through the qualities of the astral body.[30]

Evil, by contrast, as Rudolf Steiner goes on to explain, refers to a lapse of the I, a person's self-referential egoism affecting his relationship to the world and progressively undermining it, with consequences for the person's own life and for the world.

The basic possibility of such a weakness lies in the necessary evolutionary circumstances of human freedom:

> In order to gradually rise to freedom and autonomy in
> a conscious way, the human being had to pass through
> selfishness and egoism. He descended as soul that was
> part of the godhead, which cannot succumb to egoism.
> Something that forms part of an organism never
> conceives of itself as autonomous. If a finger were to
> imagine this, for instance, it would sunder itself from
> the hand and wither. This autonomy, to which we must
> evolve, and which only acquires its full significance
> once autonomy's fundamental quality becomes that of
> selflessness, could never have arisen if it did not start with
> selfishness. Selfishness entered the human body so that
> the human being became a selfish, egoistic being.

The petition for deliverance from evil therefore addresses true, unalienated development of the I, with full reference and connection to the world. 'It is thus that the Christian of the esoteric schools needed to petition.'[31]

Towards the end of his lecture in Berlin on January 28, 1907, Rudolf Steiner spoke as follows about the Lord's Prayer as an expression of the sevenfold human being and of the future evolutionary tasks to be undertaken in accord with the cosmos:

> Thus we find in the seven petitions of the Lord's Prayer
> nothing other than an expression of the fact that the
> human soul, if it properly rises to this, petitions divine
> will to enable the separate aspects of the human being
> to develop so that a person can find his right path in life
> through the universe, developing all aspects of his nature

in the right way. The Lord's Prayer is therefore a prayer by means of which we can, in moments when we need it, raise ourselves to the meaning of the evolution of our sevenfold human nature; and the seven petitions, even when uttered by the most naive people who cannot begin to understand them, are an expression of the spiritual-scientific view of human nature ...

There is no authentic prayer that is not born from great knowledge, and the great initiate, the founder of Christianity, Christ Jesus, was addressing the seven aspects of human nature at the moment when he taught this prayer, giving expression in it to this sevenfold nature of the human being.[32]

In Christ Jesus lived the mystery knowledge of the future – knowledge of the human being in his connection with the cosmos. Drawing on the substance of this knowledge, he was able to reverse the 'all-prevailing prayer' of the ancient mysteries, the cosmic Lord's Prayer, and reconfigure it anew, with an inner order and composition whose truth has given it an efficacy that endures through millennia.[33] As Steiner said on March 6, 1907 in Cologne, we need know no more about human nature 'than what the Lord's Prayer tells us'. In this context he continues:

It is the most effective prayer. This (sevenfold) rhythm that began to resonate in the soul, became apparent to an esoteric pupil who knew that Christ, in praying the Lord's Prayer, was praying human theosophy, and was living within prayer.[34]

According to Steiner, Christ not only gave the disciples the Lord's Prayer as an 'instruction for prayer', but prayed it for them.[35] He lived and prayed human theosophy, the human divine wisdom which is cognisant of the 'originating powers of the human being'.[36]

This human-centred theosophy and its meditative, prayerful formulation, was intended to help human beings to survive and pursue the good in the face of all powers of degeneration and decline, of sickness at the various levels of their being. In his Berlin lecture on January 28, 1907, Rudolf Steiner spoke comprehensively (albeit briefly) about this future human perspective. At one point he said: 'If the human being desires to evolve towards this, then he must have the strength to develop his higher triad and his lower triad to the point where they sustain and preserve the physical body in the proper way.'[37] The goal of human evolution is intimately bound up with preservation of the physical body, of the human form and with the 'resurrection body' of the I which Rudolf Steiner first spoke of in detail in his lectures, From Jesus to Christ, in October 1911.[38]

The fourth petition, addressing the physical body, occupies a middle position in the sevenfold composition of the Lord's Prayer. At its heart, directly preceded by an invocation of the highest principle of Creation – the Father God (Thy will be done) Rudolf Steiner shifted to the beginning of his reflections on the Lord's Prayer in 1907. From this perspective the Lord's Prayer is concerned with the redemption and continuing survival of the human being. This redemption is possible through spiritual development and is predicated on balancing all one-sidedness and thus temptation arising from polar elements of the adversarial powers.

★

Finally, in the autumn of 1921, twelve months after the opening of the Goetheanum as a School of Spiritual Science, Rudolf Steiner spoke of inner engagement with the Lord's Prayer, to over a hundred theologians.[39] This was fourteen years – two seven-year periods – after his Lord's Prayer lectures of 1907, which were known only to a small number of his audience. In Dornach in 1921, however, Steiner was not concerned with an esoteric examination of the Lord's Prayer as practised in the hermetic schools of early Christianity, but instead with its place in a renewed Christian Mass and act of worship, which he tried to highlight to the gathered theology students and ministers of various denominations. He was thus also concerned with paths of inner life and experience, based on a true hearing of the prayer, which was to bring it inwardly alive in the sound of words. Steiner had been emphasizing the importance of this for many years in various accounts of spiritual development and of working with esoteric mantras.[40] Now he said of working with the Lord's Prayer:

> We have to journey from the concept to the word, for
> in this lies a quite different inward experience – when
> we, without speaking outwardly, do not have a merely
> abstract concept in us but instead a living experience of
> the word sound, irrespective of which language it may
> be. The whole Lord's Prayer will in a sense take away
> some of the specific nature of language, even if we do
> not merely picture the thought content in a particular
> language but invoke the word-sound content. A great
> deal of importance was assigned to this aspect of prayer
> in former times: to inner enlivening of the sound content
> of the words; for only when the sound content becomes
> inwardly alive does the prayer transform into what it
> must be: a dialogue with the divine.[41]

Properly formed speaking of the Lord's Prayer during the act of worship, with full declamatory power, aims to help people experience the inner movement of the prayer – the 'real inner dialogue with the divine' which Steiner tried to demonstrate as the structural principle of the Lord's Prayer ('A prayer will never be authentic if it is not a dialogue with the divine; and the Lord's Prayer, in its distinctive structure, is intended to be such a dialogue in the most eminent sense.'[42]). This dialogue, said

Steiner, lives between the poles of 'self-extinction' or surrender of one's being in devotion to the divine interlocutor and a subsequently renewed 'self-grasp' as return to and refocus on one's own I. Steiner had first described this process two years earlier, in August and October 1919, as a phenomenon (or foundation) of the sense of I (through which we have perception of 'you'): in the reactive process in which we turn to and focus on another person, temporarily 'sleeping into' him, then re-asserting ourselves again.[43] At that time Steiner had said of this 'dialogue between one person and another':

> When you meet another person, the following
> occurs: you briefly perceive the other and he makes
> an impression on you. This impression disturbs you
> inwardly. You feel that the person, who is really a
> being such as you are yourself, is launching an attack
> upon you. This makes you defend yourself inwardly,
> opposing this attack, becoming inwardly aggressive
> towards the other. This aggressive aspect weakens again
> and ceases; and then the other person can once again
> make an impression on you. This means you have
> time to increase your power of aggression, and again
> you become aggressive. You weaken again in this, and
> once more the other makes an impression on you, and
> so forth. This is the relationship that exists when one
> person encounters another and perceives the I of the
> other. Devotion to the person – then inner self-defence;
> devotion to the other – inner self-defence: sympathy –
> antipathy; sympathy – antipathy. I am not now talking of
> feeling life but only of the perception in each encounter.
> The soul vibrates in sympathy – antipathy, sympathy
> – antipathy. As sympathy develops, you sleep into the
> other person; as antipathy develops, you wake up again,
> and so on. This is a very rapid alternation, vibrating,
> between waking and sleeping when we encounter

another person. That this happens is something we owe
to the organ of the sense of I.[44]

Steiner speaks here of a 'pendulum movement' that uncon-
sciously occurs in the sphere of human will:

Sleeping into the other, awakening in ourselves, we
thereby once more fall asleep in the other and awaken
in ourselves again. And this complex process that
oscillates back and forth between sleeping into the other
and awakening in ourselves, takes place whenever we
encounter another person. This is a process that occurs
in our will. We do not perceive it only because we do not
perceive our will at all.[45]

A dialogue with the divine likewise occurs in a comparable way,
as Steiner makes clear two years later in his course for theologians.
The Lord's Prayer starts with 'reverent contemplation' as we
turn to the 'ground of the world,' to the origins of all being, to
the creative, spiritual principle of the cosmos: Our Father, who
art in the heavens.[46]

The heavens are, basically, the totality of the cosmos, and
by saying Our Father in the heavens, we make tangible
for ourselves the fact that the principle we are addressing
here is permeated by spirit: we turn to the spirit. That is
the perception, the thing we ought to make as tangible
as possible for ourselves when we speak the phrase Our
Father in the heavens.[47]

According to Rudolf Steiner, by speaking this invocation or
inwardly hearing this phrase, we emerge from our own being.
We step beyond the conditions of our own inner existence, just
as we do in speaking or hearing the petition Thy kingdom come;
but not, by contrast, in the invocation that stands between our

turning to the heavens and the petition for the kingdom to come, which is to do with hallowing or consecration of the name:

> When we speak phrases such as Our Father, who art in the heavens or May thy kingdom come to us, we are in a sense outside ourselves. At these moments we forget ourselves by bringing these phrases to inner life and audibility within us. To a high degree we extinguish ourselves in these phrases through their content, but take ourselves in hand once again when we read or bring inwardly to life phrases that are different in structure. We take ourselves immediately in hand again when we say Hallowed be thy name.

Steiner says further of the way in which we 'grasp hold of ourselves' here:

> This Hallowed be thy name immediately transforms in us into inner deed. On the one hand we have the perception Our Father who art in the heavens: we cannot experience the full dimensions of this phrase unless something happens in us at the same time. And in tuning ourselves to inward hearing, this inner hearing calls up the name of Christ in us as in pre-Christian times the name of Yahweh was called up ... Therefore if we speak within us the phrase Our Father who art in the heavens in the right way, today, in our modern era, the name of Christ mingles with this utterance, and then we give an inner response to what we experience as a question: May this name be hallowed by us.

In explanation Steiner adds:

> It might strike you as odd when I say that the words Hallowed be thy name call forth the Christ name in us.

But, my dear friends, therein lies the whole secret of Christ. This Christ-secret will not be properly regarded until people rightly understand the beginning of the Gospel of John. At the start of the John Gospel you read the words: 'All things were made by the Word, and without the Word was not anything made that was made'. If we ascribe the creation of the universe to the Father God, we transgress against the Gospel of John. We only read the John Gospel aright if we know that what arose, the world we have around us, arose through the Word, and thus in the Christian sense through the Christ, the Son; that the Father is the underlying substance, the ground of being, and that the Father has no name but that his name is in fact what lives in the Christ. The whole secret of Christ lies in this Hallowed be thy name, for the name of the Father is given in that of the Son.

...

And again, when we lose ourselves in the phrase May thy kingdom come to us, we find ourselves, take ourselves in hand once more by pledging that when these kingdoms come and take effect in us, divine will can truly unfold not only in heavenly realms but also here on earth where we are.

May we enact your will in our life as you, Father, have enshrined it in our inmost heart and soul.

★

The person praying or meditating the Lord's Prayer returns from this experience of dialogue with the divine, spiritual world to earthly existence – to the four stages of the second part of the prayer that unfold in the context of what has been experienced: 'This dialogue is essential to make you inwardly ready and worthy to connect what belongs to the earth with what you invoked in the dialogue, to realize it also in earthly conditions.'[48] Here, continues Rudolf Steiner, it is a matter of introducing divine, spiritual forces into the different state of earthly existence, or to develop awareness of their action within earthly conditions:

> Give us this day our everyday bread. This means that merely natural processes, and what works in us as such, should become a spiritual process through our awareness, through our inner experience. And in the same way our outlook should be transformed. We should become capable of forgiving those who have done something that harms us. We can only do so if we become aware that we ourselves have done much harm to the divine realm of spirit, and that we must therefore petition for the right outlook and stance to cope properly with what has harmed us on earth, the debt incurred in relation to us on earth. This we can only do by realizing that simply by our natural existence we continually injure the divine, and therefore always need forgiveness from the being we have incurred a debt towards.

In the Esoteric Lord's Prayer, Rudolf Steiner formulated the fifth petition as follows.[49]★

> Let our mercy toward others atone
> for the sins perpetrated upon our being.

In this way, accomplishing the dialogue with the divine enables us to configure our I-you relationships on earth in a new and different way and to reconnect the earth sphere with the cosmic realm of spirit in the social domain. The 'new mystery prayer' addresses the community of human beings, the beings of nature, and the divine hierarchies. This reconnection of the human being with the Fathers in the heavens alters social interaction:

If we increasingly approach the Lord's Prayer with such feelings, my dear friends, then this prayer will deepen into an inner experience that enables us, through the mood we thereby engender in ourselves, to create the possibility not only of physical interactions between people but interactions between one human soul and another. For you see, in a sense we then bring ourselves into connection with the divine and find divine Creation in the other; and only then do we learn to sense how we should understand a phrase such as: 'What you have done to the least of my brothers you have done to me also.' Then we have learned to feel the divine in all earthly existence.[50]

The transformation of substance is a dimension of Christ's activity on earth – and no less so is the ordering of destiny, of social balance. Frieling wrote:

In the realm of the solar heart of Christ, one bears another's burden. True community becomes apparent where debt or trespass is transformed into love through forgiveness. Forgiveness is not merely extinguishing or erasing but is something positive, a gift. We can only forgive if we possess an inner wealth, are capable of loving evil into good.[51]

This process can and must be accomplished on earth. At the same time it shapes our after-death existence in an era when Rudolf Steiner said Christ will become the Lord of human destiny.[52] He sustains and orders relationships between human beings after they enter the world of spirit. The fifth petition seeks to enable this world of spirit, also its social forces, to gain access to the earthly world: Let our mercy toward others atone for the sins perpetrated upon our being.

Steiner said to the theologians in relation to the phrases about temptation and evil:

Lead us not into temptation means: let our connection
with you be so alive that we do not succumb to
dissolution in merely natural existence, giving ourselves
up to mere creaturely life; and allow us to hold fast to you
in all our daily nourishment. And liberate us, deliver us
from evil. Evil consists in the human being's separation
or sundering from the divine; we ask that we be liberated
and delivered from this evil.[53]

Thus is accomplished the real reversal of what Jesus, in
preparation for the future step brought about by the Jordan
baptism, experienced in the ancient mysteries as the tragedy of
earthly incarnation and the action of evil, sickness and demonic
power in the decline of the mysteries. The Lord's Prayer invokes
a Christ-permeation of earthly existence and the transformation
of all levels of being and realms of life. Confrontation with the
powers of temptation was one of the things that Rudolf Steiner
made the central focus of the mystery building he created, the
first Goetheanum: he described the recognition, confrontation
and overcoming of evil as a decisive task of the present and
future.[54] Deliver us to our true, divinely intended form, and
let us speak the 'I am' in accord with Christ. This, according to
Frieling, is the content of the seventh and concluding petition
of the Lord's Prayer.[55] The achievement of this 'true human
form' of the 'I am' understood in both a Johannine and Pauline
manner, which can be expressed as 'I live, yet no longer I but
Christ in me' is the foundation and goal of all that Rudolf Steiner
inaugurated in Dornach.[56] At the laying of the foundation stone
for the first Goetheanum he had spoken the macrocosmic Lord's
Prayer of the ancient mystery centres, the point of departure for
the transformation that the building, its form and all labours
undertaken in it were intended to serve. So that the good may
prevail.

★

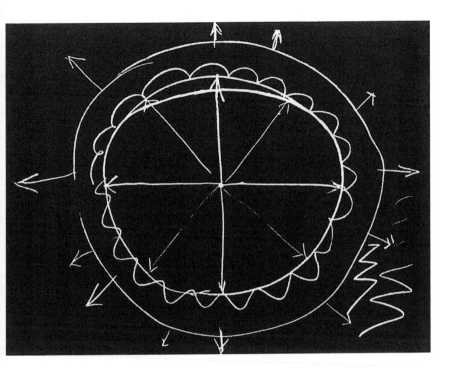

Board drawing by Rudolf Steiner, June 16, 1921. (GA 342, p. 210)

In 1921, during an early gathering in Stuttgart of the group of
theologians that founded the Christian Community one-and-a-
half years later, Rudolf Steiner discussed the concluding words
of the Lord's Prayer, the doxology, in a longer commentary on
spiritual history:

> Today, my dear friends, the form of the Lord's Prayer
> imparted in congregations is the one we find in the
> Gospel of Matthew. It ends thus: and deliver us from
> evil; for thine is the kingdom, the power and the glory for
> ever. Amen. No one who gives instruction on the Lord's
> Prayer understands this final phrase. The customary
> approach to the Gnosis, to spiritualized Christianity,

has scattered confusion over our understanding of
this last phrase. What does it mean? In the mysteries
in which it originated, this conclusion was connected
with a particular symbol, with a carrying of its whole
meaning over into symbolic representation. The symbol
established for the 'kingdom' was this [board drawing].
The boundary is the symbol for the kingdom, which
encompasses a certain area or realm. But it only makes
sense to speak of the kingdom if we delineate its limits,
depicting where it extends to.

Such a kingdom only signifies something, though, if
it is not just a limited area but is permeated with power.
Strength or power must reside at the centre, and it must
shine through the kingdom. In the realm of the kingdom,
therefore, you have something spreading outwards.
'Power' is the strength that radiates from the central
point. The radiating strength that governs or holds sway
over the kingdom is the power. All this, however, would
unfold within. If only this existed, the 'kingdom' with the
'power' would be self-contained and self-encompassed.
It which only figures in the perception of the rest of the
world, and is only present for other beings, when the
emanating quality penetrates to the surface and from
there into its wider surroundings; and is thus what shines
out into the world, is a brilliance upon the exterior
surface, is as 'glory'. The emanation from within is the
power, while the radiance of this power at the surface,
and spreading in further effulgence from it, is the glory.
If you study the form and structure of this, it can
certainly lead us to a tangible idea of what we can
conceive by the ideas of kingdom, power and glory.

Then we can seek in external reality, too, what we have
before us in soul-spiritual vision. What we had grasped as
inner perception, as mathesis, we seek also in the outer
world and find it in the sun; for that is the image.

And instead of concluding with the words of the evangelical Lord's Prayer, For thine is the kingdom, the power and the glory, you can also end the Lord's Prayer like this: For thine is the sun.

[In former times] every entity was seen in terms of the Trinity. Those who still have an inkling of real Gnostic insight know that the end of the Lord's Prayer was uttered in a way that gave expression in words to the aspects of the solar Trinity; and that, in concluding the Lord's Prayer with its seven petitions, people were conscious of praying this: '... deliver us from evil: for thou, who livest in the sun, thou art the one who is capable of so doing.' There was general awareness and perception of the fact that external nature is not unspiritual and the means to really bring to mind this spirit-permeation of the world was found by seeing the action of the Trinity everywhere ... We need to develop again this perception of reality around us as spirit-permeated. Without this perception it is utterly impossible to create the dynamic foundation of religion And if you wish to give verbal utterance to worship, then you need to gradually emerge into a grasp of the outer world. You have to be able to see objectified power, kingdom and glory in the sun.

What is thus expressed almost everywhere in the Gospels must be seen as a form of language in which the Word flows consciously into what the spirit has created externally in the world. Only when you can imbue yourself with this awareness will you really understand the Gospels. Only by considering this fully will we see how far removed modern science is from actual reality, despite people thinking they are so realistic in outlook. You see, perception of reality grew muddied and obscured in views such as those of the concluding words of the Lord's Prayer so that anyone who conflates the concept of the sun with

the concept of Christ is regarded as a heathen And a time
came when all insight into the relationship of the human
soul with reality was lost ...

Today we have reached a point when we elicit a
polemical response if we suggest that, in the Lord's
Prayer, Thine is the kingdom, the power and the glory
for all aeons, Amen points inwardly, in reality, to the
soul-spiritual Christ, and outwardly to what corresponds
to Christ in the external world: the sun. Bringing
together as one the Trinity of the kingdom, the power
and the glory as outward reality in For thine is the sun,
we can perceive the corresponding inner, soul-spiritual
reality; and address the Father, the ground of the world
in these terms: For thine is the Son, Christ Jesus, he is
with thee.[57]

Recollecting these words by Rudolf Steiner, Rittelmeyer –
who was still a Lutheran pastor in Berlin when Steiner gave this
lecture in the summer of 1921, and later became the first leader
of the Christian Community – wrote:

When Rudolf Steiner spoke of the concluding words of
the Lord's Prayer, he drew on his spiritual research in
saying that originally these concluding words were: For
thine is the sun! These mysterious words are such that we
can only make something of them by reflecting further
on them ourselves. One day I realized that these three
last words of the Lord's Prayer correspond precisely to
the ascending hierarchy of the three sun worlds: Thine
is the kingdom – here we are in the realm of the creating
spirits, the Exusiai. Thine is the power – here we enter
the realm of the spirits who permeate the cosmos with
strength or energy, the Dynamis. Thine is the glory – this
is the realm of the light-imbuing, illumining spirits, the
Kyriotetes. We are in the solar realm: Thine is the sun![58]

To conclude, let us continue with the passage just cited:

> Bringing together as one the Trinity of the kingdom, the
> power and the glory as outward reality in For thine is
> the sun, we can perceive the corresponding inner, soul-
> spiritual reality; and address the Father, the ground of the
> world in these terms: For thine is the Son, Christ Jesus,
> he is with thee.

An Egyptian amulet inscription, the only extant testimony
to early Christian texts, ends the Lord's Prayer, instead of with
the doxology, with the invocation O Lord Christ![59] In his High
Priestly Prayer Christ petitioned the Father, 'I desire that they
also ... may ... behold my glory which thou hast given me' (John
17:24). This vision of the glory or doxa of Christ (prefigured on
Mount Tabor) came about subsequently in reality through the
events of the Resurrection, Ascension and Whitsun.[60] In the first
chapter of his Gospel, John wrote:

> And we have beheld his revelation,
> the revelation of the only Son of the Father,
> full of grace and truth. (John 1:14 M)

Notes

The quotations by Rudolf Steiner have been translated from the German. The reference is to the German volume Nos. of the Gesamtausgabe (GA). The bibliography shows English translations where they exist.

Introduction

1 Guardini, *Das Gebet des Herrn,* p. 9.
2 Aquinas, *Das Vaterunser,* p. 119; GA 96, p. 210; GA97, p. 94.
3 Notes by Camille Wandrey of a question-and-answer session with Rudolf Steiner on the Lord's Prayer (Oslo, June 1912). Rudolf Steiner Archive, Dornach.
4 Compare Selg, *Christ and the Disciples.*
5 Paracelsus, *Das Mahl des Herrn,* p. 80.
6 Kelber, 'Christus im Vaterunser,' p. 79.
7 Also compare Rittelmeyer, *Das Vaterunser.* pp. 40f.
8 Thomas Aquinas, p. 119
9 Kelber, 'Christus im Vaterunser,' pp. 81f. Paracelsus also wrote: 'For we cannot say "Our Father" unless we are his sons ... Only those can say "Our Father" who have been born out of the spirit for a second time. The same holds true when Christ says, "My Father!" insofar as he is born from God through the Word that became flesh. In this Word we too become flesh and blood. Those who are born out of this Word – that is, out of this spirit – are brothers of Christ and can say, "Our Father" .' *(Das Mahl des Herrn,* p. 77).
10 Althoff, *Das Vaterunser,* p. 13.
11 GA 97, p. 107
12 GA 343, p.151
13 GA 211, p. 189

1. Respect for this Prayer

1 GA 148, p. 38.
2 GA 148, p. 38.
3 'During his childhood and youth, my father was in the closest contact

with a Premonstratensian order in Geras. He always looked back upon this phase of his life with great affection. He liked telling us about the work he had done there and how the monks had instructed him.' (GA 28, p. 8).

4 This and the following quote from Steiner, *Selbstzeugnisse. Autobiographische Dokumente,* p. 19.

5 Rudolf Steiner reiterates the importance for him of attending services in Neudörfl near the end of his autobiography: 'Of my boyhood in Neudörfl, I retained a strong sense of how observing the services and their festive musical offerings allows the riddles of existence to rise up in one in a strongly suggestive way. The Bible and Catechism lessons that the priest gave us had far less effect upon my soul than what he enacted by conducting services that mediated between sensory and supersensible worlds. From the beginning, all this was not mere outward form for me, but a profound experience. This was all the truer since it set me at odds with my parental home. The life I had absorbed in religious services did not leave me again when I returned to my own domestic surroundings..' (GA 28, p. 28).

6 See GA 28, p. 125 ff; see also Bock, *The Life and Times of Rudolf Steiner,* Vol. 1, pp. 54–56; and Meyer, *Rudolf Steiners 'eigenste Mission',* pp. 34ff.

7 Compare testimonies in the study by Lindenberg, *Individualismus und offenbare Religion.*

8 Letter to Rosa Mayreder, Nov 19, 1891 in GA 39, p. 124. GA 258, pp. 66ff.

9 GA 28, p. 366.

10 Marie Steiner-von Sivers: 'Wendepunkte des Geisteslebens,' p. 16. Rudolf Steiner himself reported this conversation as follows: 'At the time when Frl von Sivers was already a member [of the Theosophical Society], I myself not yet however, a conversation once took place between us in which she asked why I had not joined the society. I replied to her at length, in words I can here summarize: it will always be impossible for me to belong to a society that pursues a form of theosophy that is as permeated by uncomprehending oriental mysticism as is the case in the present Theosophical Society. My vocation, you see, would be to acknowledge that there are more significant esoteric impulses for our times; and it would be impossible, given this insight, to accept that the Occident has something to learn from such oriental-type mysticism. What I must represent would be exposed to false appraisal if I were to say that I wish to be a member of a society that makes oriental-type mysticism its shibboleth. That was the content of our conversation.' (GA 264, p. 406).

11 On one occasion (on April 16, 1905) Rudolf Steiner wrote to Marie von Sivers as follows about a theosophical lecture tour he gave: 'In Munich, things seemed to me to go very well again. But the lectures which have a Christian theme – such as the one about the apostle Paul

– meet with a poorer response. There are two difficulties here. Firstly, the theosophical movement has so far developed in a way that makes people regard theosophy as something essentially Indian, and so they do not think a theosophist has anything to say about Christianity. And secondly, official Christianity today appears in a form that makes it hard to give credence to its true nature, as I present it. Various further steps will be needed to create more clarity here. Catholicism no longer finds the words to convey the nature of Christ because it has distanced itself from modern forms of thinking and therefore can really only now be understood by those whose lack of education means that they have not yet come into contact with these forms of thought. Protestantism is in the process of losing the Christ altogether, due to the rationalism and factual historicism practised by its theologians. Instead it holds fast only to Jesus of Nazareth, seeking to relate this "plain and humble" figure to modern views of democracy. This is why the non-theosophists were somewhat at a loss in Karlsruhe at my public lecture on Christianity, while the theosophists greeted it warmly but also with some surprise. One could tell that they had no previous inkling that Christianity could contain a theosophy of this kind.' (GA 262, p. 105).

12   Letter from Marie von Sivers to Edouard Schuré on Jan 13, 1907. Quoted in Wiesberger, *Marie Steiner-von Sivers,* p. 191.

13   For more on this hint and its karmic dimension, see Meyer, *Rudolf Steiners 'eigenste Mission',* pp. 77ff.

14   Quoted in Wiesberger, *Marie Steiner-von Sivers,* p. 193.

15   GA 100, p. 87.

16   In particular GA 96, 97, 99 and 100.

17   Compare for instance, Selg: *'Ich bleibe bei Ihnen.'*

18   GA 262, p. 26.

19   Compare Wiesberger, *Rudolf Steiners esoterische Lehrtätigkeit,* pp. 251–67, and Krause-Zimmer, *Christian Rosenkreutz.*

20   Compare GA 59, pp. 168ff.

21   'If one surveys the wealth of literature on prayer and the Lord's Prayer, one finds that his [Rudolf Steiner's] accounts stand head and shoulders above all other such writings. You get the sense that this is someone who really *knows* what he is talking about. At the same time you realize that this is someone who is not only able to speak *about* prayer but has direct experience of what it means to pray. These are the words of someone who *prays.* Actual experience and intimate knowledge are required to speak about prayer in this way.' (Schroeder, *Das Gebet,* pp. 111f).

22   GA 59, pp. 130f.

23   GA 59, p. 126.

24   GA 96, p. 204.

25   Compare comments by Hella Wiesberger on the term 'mantra' in Rudolf Steiner's work in *Rudolf Steiners esoterische Lehrtätigkeit,* pp. 63ff.

26   GA 97, pp. 92, 103. Althoff wrote as follows about the mantric charac-

ter of the Lord's Prayer *(Das Vaterunser,* pp. 20f): 'At least the first half of the words of the Lord's Prayer are by nature invocations: mantric invocations that not only have a significance we can reflect upon and that fill our sensibility with reverence and awe, but additionally are words that work through their very essence, bearing intrinsic power in the original sense of the Word (Logos). These are words that call forth actual being and give it reality.'

27 GA 266/2, p. 26.

28 Verbal report by Kurt Walther (1874–1940). Schroeder even said that Rudolf Steiner 'prayed the Lord's Prayer aloud *every day' (Das Gebet,* p. 97, no source given, emphasis added). Schroeder was very probably referring here to Rudolf Steiner's collaboration with Ita Wegman during the last phase of his life. They started their work each evening by speaking the Lord's Prayer in the studio. Speaking the prayer in this way as 'new mystery prayer' marked the start of their shared work in a task connected with the 'new mysteries' in the medical domain. They spoke the prayer together when Rudolf Steiner was in Dornach and was able to work with Ita Wegman. To my knowledge there is no account of Steiner speaking the Lord's Prayer *every day* in Berlin, but we must remember that Steiner was not there every day (at 17 Motzstrasse) because of his many lecture tours.

29 GA 97, p. 114.

30 Notes by Camille Wandrey of a question-and-answer session with Rudolf Steiner on the Lord's Prayer (Oslo, June 1912). Rudolf Steiner Archive, Dornach.

31 Compare for instance, the essays by Rudolf Frieling, 'Das Vaterunser mit den Verstorbenen gebetet' (in *Der erneuerte christliche Gottesdienst,* pp. 118–24) and Alfred Schütze: 'Das Vaterunser und die Toten' (in Rau, *Wege zum Beten,* pp. 92–97). Compare also Schroeder, *Das Gebet,* pp. 82ff.

32 Rittelmeyer, *Rudolf Steiner Enters my Life,* p. 57. In relation to the concept and content of the 'Fifth Gospel', see GA 148 and Selg, *Rudolf Steiner and the Fifth Gospel.*

33 GA 300a, p. 81.

34 GA 300a, p. 96.

35 Martha Haebler: 'Rudolf Steiner in einer Waldorfschulklasse' in *Erziehungskunst,* 1952, No. 12, p. 359.

36 Rudolf Treichler: 'Ein Besuch Dr Steiners in meiner Englisch-Stunde,' in Heydebrand, *Rudolf Steiner in der Waldorfschule,* p. 102.

37 See Heidenreich, *Growing Point,* and Gädeke, R. *Die Gründer der Christengemeinschaft.*

38 GA 344, p. 85f.

39 GA 59, p. 131.

40 Quoted in Gädeke, W. *Anthroposophie und die Fortbildung der Religion,* p. 177. Compare also the essay by Emil Bock: 'Gebet und Kultus'. In: Rau, *Wege zum Beten,* pp. 56–64.

41 Rudolf Steiner gave the Russian artist Tatyana Kisseleff (1881–1970) forms for presenting the Lord's Prayer in eurythmy, and practised these with her ('He wanted the prayer to be done in Latin in eurythmy. He himself recited it, very slowly') Kisseleff's brief account of their collaboration (in 1914) is very striking. She said that the version of the Lord's Prayer rehearsed according to Steiner's suggestions was only performed in eurythmy on one occasion, in Latin (with *panem nostrum supersubstantialem* instead of *panem nostrum quotidianum*, compare Note 40 of Ch. 3). This was on Dec 22, 1918 at the branch premises of the Anthroposophical Society in Basel, before the Christmas tree (Kisseleff, *Eurythmische Arbeit,* pp. 66f). In the years after Steiner's death, according to Edwin Fröböse, Marie Steiner-von Sivers frequently worked with the speech chorus at the Goetheanum on the text of the 'esoteric Lord's Prayer', and occasionally performed this: 'It was spoken on very special occasions' (GA 268, p. 271).

42 See Emmichoven, W. 'Das Vaterunser' in *Der Grundstein*, pp. 64–71.

43 See Emmichoven, E. *Wer war Ita Wegman,* Vol. 1, p. 243 (also Vol. 2, pp. 374f).

44 As Madeleine van Deventer told Emanuel Zeylmans van Emmichoven in 1981, during the last phase of his illness, Ita Wegman helped Rudolf Steiner to stand up to say the Lord's Prayer.

45 As cited by Ita Wegman, 'Das Krankenlager, die letzten Tage und Stunden Dr Steiners,' *Das Goetheanum*, April 19, 1925. (Reprinted in Wegman, *An die Freunde,* and Wegman, *Erinnerung an Rudolf Steiner.*

46 According to verbal accounts, including that of Daniel von Bemmelen (1899–1982), Rudolf Steiner (also?) spoke the Lord's Prayer in Latin in his studio. But see also Emmichoven, E, *Wer war Ita Wegman.* Vol. 2, p. 374.

47 GA 266/I, p. 198. Shortly before this, on Jan 19, 1907, Rudolf Steiner stressed the following in Stuttgart: 'Prayers in ancient languages lose their old power when translated into modern languages. There is much more power in the Latin words of the *Pater noster* than in the Lord's Prayer. The original Lord's Prayer is in Aramaic. Those who spoke it in Aramaic, felt its magical potency.' (GA 97, p. 99).

48 Marie Steiner transcribed the text in two notebooks *before* 1913 (Rudolf Steiner Archive, Dornach. The literary estate of Marie Steiner-von Sivers).

49 GA 268, p. 370.

50 At the cremation of Caroline Wilhelm in Basel, Oct 27, 1920. As documented in the shorthand script by Helene Finckh (Notebook No. 4276), Hugo Schuster spoke the Esoteric Lord's Prayer in the second part of the funeral service, instead of the usual wording (Rudolf Steiner Archive, Dornach. Noted by Wolfgang Gädeke).

51 See Michael Debus, 'Der Totenkultus und die anthroposophische Bewegung' in Debus & Kacer, *Das Handeln im Umkreis des Todes*, pp.

15f. In relation to the whole context, see also Selg, *The Path of the soul after Death.*

52 Quoted in Emmichoven, E. *Wer war Ita Wegman,* Vol. 2, p. 374.

53 It is conceivable, however, that the wording of the Esoteric Lord's Prayer was only spoken at the beginning of their collaboration, and that after falling ill Rudolf Steiner spoke the prayer in the original words (or even in Latin, see Note 46 above) on which he based his addresses to the theologians (and the Act of Consecration of Man of The Christian Community). It is probably going too far to describe the wording of the Esoteric Lord's Prayer as a version 'more advanced in terms of esoteric knowledge' (Poeppig, *Das Vaterunser).* Rudolf Steiner himself never used such a formulation or interpretation.

54 GA 268, p. 341. In relation to the missing fifth petition ('Let our mercy toward others atone for the sins perpetrated upon our being') in the various transcripts of the Esoteric Lord's Prayer, compare the editor's note in GA 268, p. 371, and Note 49 of Ch. 4. The version in Ita Wegman's notebook also lacks this petition. The text noted by Wegman runs (in English translation) as follows: 'Our Father, Father, you who were, are, and will be in our inmost being. May your name be glorified in us all and praised. May your kingdom grow more expansive in our deeds and in the conduct of our lives. May we enact your will as you, Father, have enshrined it in our inmost soul. In overflowing abundance you give us spiritual nourishment, the bread of life, through all changing conditions of our lives. You do not allow the tempter to work in us beyond the capacity of our strength – for no temptation can prevail in your being, Father, and the tempter is only appearance and delusion, from which you deliver us, Father, through the light of your knowledge. May your power and glory work in us through all cycles of time. Amen.' (Ita Wegman Archive, Arlesheim).

2. Lord, Teach us to Pray

1 Althoff, *Das Vaterunser,* p. 19

2 Mark also (in chapter 6, following the account of the return of the disciples after being sent out) records the community of Christ's disciples 'sitting down together' in a 'quiet place' in a concentrated and prayerful stance (Mark 6:31f). Rudolf Frieling commented on this scene as follows: 'When they returned, Christ said: "Come away by yourselves to a lonely place, and rest a while." For many were coming and going, and they did not find time even to eat. And so they journeyed over the lake with Christ and seek out a lonely place where they can be "by themselves". The Greek words *kat idian* means that they come fully to "themselves", to their "authentic nature". They are introduced to the conduct of inner life. The suggestion is that uninterrupted external demands would overtax them. The Greek word for "rest" also

contains the idea of "pause", here connected with the prefix *ana*, thus "upwards". It is intended to be a really "creative pause", in which they open to a higher realm.' *(Gesammelte Schriften,* Vol. 3, pp. 110f).

3   Rittelmeyer, *Das Vaterunser,* p. 22.

4   GA 97, p. 85.

5   Bock, *Das Evangelium,* p. 675.

6   Frieling wrote: 'The evangelist's little phrase, "as he made pause," gives us insight into how such a thing actually occurred. A longer period of contemplation and meditation includes pauses. At such a moment, the request of a disciple witnessing Christ's prayer causes him to give the Lord's Prayer to his followers. In the Gospel of Luke are preserved the diverse contexts in which Christ spoke his words, and which gave rise to them. This is also true of the moment at which the fundamental Christian prayer was first revealed. Luke allows us to witness how this prayer is rooted in Christ's experiences of inward communing, and subsequently was further elaborated into its fully-fledged form as Matthew conveys it.' *(Gesammelte Schriften,* Vol. 3, p. 113).

7   Rittelmeyer, *Das Vaterunser,* p. 14 f.

8   Frieling, *Gesammelte Schriften,* Vol. 3, p. 203. ('From his communing with the divine, Christ draws the strength to bring his supersensible light form to such strong expression that, to use an expression of Rilke, it 'dawns upon the face' of the watching disciples.' pp. 112f.)

9   In relation to this, see Frieling, *Gesammelte Schriften,* Vol. 3, pp. 113–15.

10 Frieling, *Gesammelte Schriften,* Vol. 3, p. 111.

11 Althoff, *Das Vaterunser,* p. 24.

12 Althoff, *Das Vaterunser,* p. 19. Aquinas, *Das Vaterunser,* p. 129. Compare also Selg, *Mysterium cordis,* pp. 92ff.

13 In contrast to the overwhelming majority of academics and theologians who (like Rudolf Steiner also) assumed the original language of the Lord's Prayer to be Aramaic (compare Cullmann, *Das Gebet im neuen Testament,* p. 53 on the available literature), Althoff held the view that the prayer was originally in Greek. 'In its original form it [the Lord's Prayer] arose in the world language of the Christian message, in Greek' *(Das Vaterunser,* p. 12). Althoff sought to demonstrate this by detailed study of the constituent elements of the prayer's wording, applicable only to the Greek version. His studies are significant in content and of lasting cultural-historical value. They include his commentaries on problems of textual tradition *(Das Vaterunser,* pp. 26–49) which deal with the currency of Aramaic, Hebrew and Greek in Palestine at the time of Christ, and the distinctive nature of Greek in the evolution of human consciousness – also in relation to the Jewish people and the spirit of the Hebrew language. Although the main thrust of Althoff's thesis is very likely unsustainable – as can already be seen from the numerous *Abba* evocations in the letters of Paul – his commentary not only contributes a great deal to our understanding of the Lord's Prayer

but also illumines the special relationship of the Christ event to the Greek spirit and the pre-Christian Michael epoch. The Christ event was able to unfold in the 'body' of the Greek language in a unique way: in a certain respect it was created or shaped for this.

14 Althoff, *Das Vaterunser,* p. 20.
15 Rittelmeyer, *Das Vaterunser,* p. 52.
16 Aquinas, *Das Vaterunser,* p. 126–28.
17 Aquinas, *Das Vaterunser,* p. 144.
18 Aquinas, *Das Vaterunser,* p. 136.
19 Althoff, *Das Vaterunser,* p. 71.
20 Compare Selg, *Christ and the Disciples.*
21 Rittelmeyer, *Das Vaterunser,* p. 93.
22 In his exegesis of the sixth petition of the Lord's Prayer, Paracelsus stressed that Peter himself did not pray to be preserved from temptation, and therefore denied Christ. 'Peter never ... asked to be safeguarded from temptation, and therefore he fell.' *(Mahl des Herrn,* p. 90).
23 Compare GA 148 and Selg, *Rudolf Steiner und das Fünfte Evangelium,* pp. 98ff.
24 For more on the development and nature of Rudolf Steiner's commentaries on the childhood of Jesus, compare the study by Hella Krause-Zimmer, 'Wann begann Rudolf Steiner über die zwei Jesusknaben zu sprechen und wie klangen seine Darstellungen des Themas vorher?' in *Mitteilungen aus der anthroposophischen Arbeit in Deutschland,* No. 163, 1988, pp. 28–41.
25 Compare GA 148; Selg, *Rudolf Steiner und das Fünfte Evangelium,* pp. 50ff; Wagner, *Die unbekannten Jahre Jesu.*
26 This and the following quotations are from GA 148, pp. 64, 293, 137, 82, 252, 292, 251.
27 GA 264, p. 259.
28 GA 148, pp. 292, 251 f.
29 Compare Emmichoven, E. *Who was Ita Wegman,* Vol. 4.
30 GA 266/I, p. 177.
31 GA 268, p. 21
32 GA 148, p. 259.
33 GA 148, p. 298
34 Compare Selg, *Das Ereignis der Jordantaufe.*
35 GA 148, p. 50f.
36 Rudolf Frieling wrote as follows about Christ Jesus' inner situation during the forty days in the wilderness: 'The experience of the Jordan baptism clearly signified such a mighty intervention in Jesus of Nazareth's consciousness and whole being that he required some time to find his way into his new existence. He could not immediately begin to act in the world. For forty days he tarried alone in the desert. Here the evangelists use expressions that strike us almost as inappropriate in relation to Christ Jesus. According to Matthew (4:1), "Then

Jesus was led up by the Spirit" from the Jordan basin to the mountains of Judea. According to Luke (4:1f) he departed from the Jordan "full of the Holy Spirit ... and was led by the Spirit ... in the wilderness." The Greek imperfect tense, "he was led," indicates a repeating condition lasting some time. One might say that the spirit "compelled him to move around in the desert" – but this was not, on the other hand, the kind of restlessness we are familiar with in states of worry and agitation. What drove Christ to wander hither and thither was the wealth or surfeit of spirit influx he had received. This had not yet come to rest within him but surged up and down and was at risk of bursting the tight vessel of human nature. The evangelist Mark expresses this in powerful, somewhat drastic terms: "The Spirit immediately drove him into the wilderness" (1:12). Nowhere else in the Gospels do we read of Jesus being "passively led" or even "driven". Elsewhere we see him only as the sovereign lord of his actions and also of his suffering, in the tranquillity and majesty of his "I am". Clearly this inner mastery first had to be achieved after the Jordan baptism. The baptized Christ Jesus needed to withdraw for those forty days in order to come to terms with what had happened to him. It is precisely because he has not fully mastered the baptism experience, and his inner state has not yet stabilized, that he experiences the influences of the adversary which, according to Matthew and Luke, were at work throughout this whole period until at last the three great temptations had been quelled. The fact, too, that Christ draws here on old sacred texts in the Bible – "it is written" – shows that the I has not yet entirely encompassed the fullness of spirit and that Christ is not yet speaking in his own full sovereignty. But from then on, after victory is achieved, such expressions of "passivity" no longer figure. Now "Jesus returned in the power of the Spirit into Galilee" (Luke 4:14).' (Frieling, *Gesammelte Schriften,* Vol. 3, pp. 107f). For more on the 'temptations' or confrontations with the adversary powers, compare Rudolf Steiner's differentiated accounts in GA 148, and my summary of the relevant passages in *Rudolf Steiner und das Fünfte Evangelium,* pp. 85ff.

37   GA 148, p. 91.
38   This and the following quotation GA 148, pp. 92ff.
39   GA 148, p. 292,
40   GA 59, pp. 124ff.
41   GA 343, p. 88.
42   See, for example, Cullmann *Das Gebet im neuen Testament,* pp. 57f.
43   GA 203, pp. 292f.
44   GA 123, pp. 173f.
45   GA 148, p. 94.
46   GA 26, p. 14.

3. Having the Courage to Invoke the Name of the Father

1 Steiner said of the Lord's Prayer that 'we only properly understand it if we absorb its authentically Christian meaning, as it was understood by the esoteric school of Paul.' Rudolf Steiner called this insight into it the 'esoteric exegesis of the Lord's Prayer' (GA 100, pp. 83, 87). See also Note 2 of Ch. 4.

2 There is extensive secondary literature, also with reference to Jewish esotericism, concerning this Old Testament or Hebrew context of the doxology, the prayer of David at the laying of the foundation stone for the temple, which invoked the I AM God (Yahweh) as the Lord of the hierarchies. Althoff also included a subtle exploration of Cabbalistic esoteric lore relating to the ten-armed Sphere Tree (Sephirot) *(Das Vaterunser,* pp. 104ff).

3 Althoff, *Das Vaterunser,* pp. 27f.

4 Jungmann, *Christliches Beten,* p. 22.

5 Cullmann, *Urchristentum und Gottesdienst,* p. 17.

6 See Furberg, *Das Pater Noster in der Messe,* p. 25.

7 Becker & Peter, *Das Heilige Vaterunser,* p. 19.

8 Becker & Peter, *Das Heilige Vaterunser,* pb. 62f.

9 Jungmann, *Missarum sollemnia,* Vol. 2, p. 339.

10 'Who should speak it ... was the question: whether, in a way similar to the *Sanctus,* it should be spoken by the whole congregation or, like the other prayers in the *Ordo Missa,* the celebrant should speak it on behalf of the faithful. Since preparation of the individual to receive the sacrament was involved here, it seemed appropriate to directly include each individual and thus the whole congregation [that is, all baptized Christians who were taking part in the service] in the Lord's Prayer, especially since they were all fully conversant with it. This solution then became the norm in the Orient[the Eastern Church] too. Everywhere the Lord's Prayer began to be assigned to the congregation, except in the Armenian liturgy where the clerics were to sing it with outspread arms. In the Byzantine Mass, though, it became common for the choir to speak it, or just one member of the choir as representative of the whole gathering. In the old Gallican liturgy, too, the Lord's Prayer was spoken by the whole congregation, while in the rest of the West the priest celebrating Mass spoke it alone. This was likewise maintained in the African Church of St Augustin, yet with expectation of the congregation's spirited inner and also ritual participation. In the Old Spanish Mass, this participation came to expression in the *Amen* spoken as response after every section of the prayer. In the Roman Mass, too, expression is given to the fact that the Lord's Prayer belongs to all the people: the prayer is divided between the priest and the people, although not in equal portions. While the older sacraments and most of the ordines offer no hints about such divided allocation,

and Gregory the Great ... only briefly indicates that, unlike in the Greek Church, the Lord's Prayer in Rome is spoken *a solo sacerdote* [only by the priest], we do learn from the Ordo of John the archicantor, that in the seventh century, thus a long time back, a decision was taken that *Sed libera nos a malo* [deliver us from evil] should be spoken as a response by all. Thus here we find that the congregation does speak it too. It is the Communion prayer of the people.' (Jungmann, *Missarum sollemnia,* Vol. 2, pp. 347ff).

11 Furberg, *Das Pater Noster in der Messe*, p. 20.

12 Jungmann, *Missarum sollemnia*, Vol. 2, p. 341.

13 Jungmann, *Missarum sollemnia*, Vol. 2, pp. 341f.

14 Becker & Peter, *Das Heilige Vaterunser*, p. 78.

15 Furberg, *Das Pater Noster in der Messe*, p. 28.

16 Furberg, *Das Pater Noster in der Messe*, p. 13

17 'Starting with Tertullian, the Romans generally relate the petition for bread to the Eucharist; some of the Greeks do the same. This is very noticeable in a text whose literal meaning, after all, clearly indicates material bread. It is predicated on the custom whereby the faithful spoke the Lord's Prayer when receiving the sacrament, even before this prayer appears as part of the liturgy in liturgical records.' (Jungmann, *Missarum sollemnia*, Vol. 2, p. 339).

18 Jungmann, *Missarum sollemnia*, Vol. 2, p. 343.

19 This and following quotes of Tertullian from Furberg, *Das Pater Noster in der Messe*, pp. 6f.

20 *Summa theologica* III. 69, 5–4.

21 Rittelmeyer, *Das Vaterunser*, p. 105.

22 GA 175, p. 324

23 Dibelius, *Umrisse zu einer Geschichte des Gebetes*, pp. 20, 22.

24 Some ancient manuscripts have 'Thy Holy Spirit come upon us and cleanse us' instead of 'Thy kingdom come' (Luke 11:2).

25 Origen, *Über das Beten*, pp. 18f.

26 Origen, *Über das Beten*, p. 26.

27 Origen, *Über das Beten*, p. 104.

28 Origen, *Über das Beten*, p. 28.

29 Origen, *Über das Beten*, p. 31.

30 A further expositions of this theme is Wilhelm Maas, 'Zum Menschenbild des Origenes (Hegemonikon)' in Origen, *Über das Beten*, pp. 90–98.

31 Origen, *Über das Beten*, p. 33.

32 Origen, *Über das Beten*, p. 46 (see Cullmann, *Das Gebet im neuen Testament*, pp. 70ff for more on this theme). See also the remarkable commentary by Althoff *(Das Vaterunser,* pp. 80–90) in relation to the 'mystery meaning' – overlooked by Origenes – of the Greek word *epiousion*. Althoff also considered the mysteries of Eleusis, writing: 'A byname of Demeter, though one rarely used and then only with

sacred awe, is *Epiassa*, which is derived from the modified participle (feminine) *epioussa*: that is, from *ep-i-n̥-tha (n̥* is a vowelized *n* that must be read as *'ah'*). Here Demeter is experienced as the earth mother of the gods, as the 'approaching one'. In the Eleusinian mysteries, in the *epopteia*, the highest level of initiation, the ear of corn is raised above the head of the person being initiated. When the corn is ground, its body crushed and surrendered, it approaches us as in an everlasting sacrament, becoming *artos epioussios*, the gift of which we ask for 'today'. This petition becomes an invocation insofar as we work our way into the insight that in the everlasting bread Christ approaches us, revealing himself to be the bread of life.' *(Das Vaterunser*, pp. 85f).

33 In the non-Byzantine liturgies of the Eastern Church, the follow up of the Lord's Prayer underlined the last two petitions, repeating them or markedly enlarging on the text. In the St James *anaphora*, after speaking the Lord's Prayer the priest continued: 'Yes, Lord, our God, do not lead us into temptation that we should not be capable of enduring, but with temptation give us also the issue that we may prevail, and deliver us from evil.' (Jungmann, *Missarum sollemnia*, Vol. 2, p. 344).

34 Origen, *Über das Beten*, p. 63.

35 Origen, *Über das Beten*, pp. 73f.

36 Aquinas, *Das Vaterunser*, p. 157.

37 Origen, *Über das Beten*, p. 73.

38 Origen, *Über das Beten*, p. 118.

39 Althoff, *Das Vaterunser*, p. 140–93.

40 Compare Althoff, *Das Vaterunser*, p. 142 ff. The only change made by Jerome was to substitute the word *supersubstantialem* ('supersubstantial' or 'above material existence') for *quotidianum* (daily): 'the bread that is above all beings and all creatures', 'the chosen bread of Christians, that is, Christ himself' (Becker & Peter, *Das Heilige Vaterunser*, p. 7).

41 GA 325, p. 56.

42 Althoff, *Das Vaterunser*, pp. 155f.

43 Althoff, *Das Vaterunser*, p. 157.

44 GA 325, pp. 40ff.

45 GA 325, p. 39.

46 GA 213, pp. 192f.

47 GA 325, p. 45.

48 See Selg, *Christus und die Jünger*, pp. 107–16 in relation to Rudolf Steiner's commentaries on the teachings of the resurrected Christ to his disciples ('To them he presented himself alive after his passion by many proofs, appearing to them during forty days, and speaking of the kingdom of God.' Acts 1:3). On Maundy Thursday, April 13, 1922, Rudolf Steiner said in The Hague about these teachings of the resurrected Christ and the mystery wisdom conveyed in them: 'During the first four Christian centuries this knowledge remained alive in a sense. Then it ossified in the Roman Catholic Church: while this latter

retained the Mass, it no longer possessed any interpretation of it. The Mass, regarded as a continuation of the Last Supper as described in the Bible offers no meaning unless one first projects an interpretation on it. The fact that the Mass was enacted with its wonderful rite, its imitation of the four mystery chapters, is certainly based on the fact that the resurrected Christ was also the teacher of those who were able to receive these teachings in a higher esoteric way. In subsequent centuries all that remained of it was a more or less shallow teaching of the Mystery of Golgotha.' (GA 211, p. 136f).

49 GA 353, p. 96.
50 GA 351, p. 101.
51 GA 325, pp. 51, 57.
52 GA 325, lectures of May 15 and 16, 1921.

4. A Dialogue with the Divine

1 Rittelmeyer, *Das Vaterunser,* p. 22
2 GA 110, p. 26. 'The school that the Apostle Paul established was profoundly esoteric. In the outer world Christianity was presented exoterically. Paul entrusted Dionysius the Areopagite with nurturing the esoteric aspect of this wisdom.' (GA 97, p. 124). In various lectures Rudolf Steiner discussed this, frequently hinting that while the esoteric school was founded by Paul, he had primarily exoteric work to do, and handed the leadership of the school largely to Dionysius, who developed a Christian-Gnostic path of schooling (GA 99, p. 153). Paul 'founded' the school *'through Dionysius'* (GA 110, p. 27). Dionysius supervised its inner development, which proved fundamentally successful. According to Steiner, all later esoteric wisdom and schooling emerged from his esoteric school of Christianity (GA 99, p. 153). See also GA 93a, p. 97 in relation to the authenticity of pseudo-Dionysius' writings (from the sixth century) and questions regarding the person Dionysius the Areopagite himself: 'Teachings about the gods [divine hierarchies] were first systematically organized by the pupil of the Apostle Paul, *Dionysius the Areopagite.* However, they were not written down until the sixth century. Scholars therefore deny that Dionysius the Areopagite ever existed, and speak of the writings of the pseudo-Dionysius, as if old traditions or accounts were first gathered together and compiled in the sixth century. We can only ascertain the truth by reading in the Akashic Records. This tells us that Dionysius did indeed live in Athens, that he was initiated by Paul and was commissioned by him to establish the teachings of higher spirit beings and communicate these to certain other initiates. In those times certain lofty teachings were never written down but only passed on orally. In this way too, Dionysius imparted teachings about the gods to his pupils, who in turn passed them on. Each person in the direct line of this schooling was also intentionally called Dionysius, so that the last of

them, who recorded these teachings in writing, was one of the many who were all called Dionysius.'

3   GA 97, p. 142.
4   Quoted in Becker & Peter, *Das Heilige Vaterunser*, p. 126.
5   GA 97, p. 99.
6   See GA 9, pp. 51ff for more on these highest human levels.
7   Althoff, *Das Vaterunser*, p. 67: 'If one remained trapped in the accustomed ideas and feelings of ecclesiastical traditions, one would have to say: This is *not* how one ought to speak with "our Father in heaven"! But a merely "pious" stance does not in the least accord with the prayer's semantic forms, which indicate a quite different stance of prayer in which the soul practises grasping hold of itself – in full trust in the omnipresent world of the Father, but also with the utmost spiritual energy.'
8   GA 96, p. 217.
9   See especially GA 132.
10   GA 96, p. 208.
11   See GA 110.
12   GA 203, p. 300.
13   GA 196, p. 216.
14   GA 96, p. 210.
15   Compare GA 240, pp. 291f in relation to the earthly dimension of the 'life spirit' of the Christ being since the Mystery of Golgotha.
16   GA 240, p. 211.
17   Althoff, *Das Vaterunser*, p. 68f.
18   GA 167, p. 185.
19   See Wiesberger, *Rudolf Steiners esoterische Lehrtätigkeit*, pp. 58–72.
20   GA 96, pp. 217, 210f.
21   GA 97, p. 112.
22   Thomas Aquinas, *Das Vaterunser*, p. 145.
23   GA 96, p. 212. In relation to the concept of the physical body see Selg, *Vom Logos menschlicher Physis*.
24   GA 96, p. 212.
25   About the life body, see Selg, *Vom Logos menschlicher Physis*, Vol. 1, pp. 107ff.
26   GA 96, p. 214.
27   See Selg, *Rudolf Steiner and the Fundamental Social Law*.
28   'Just as physical forces emanate from the centre of the earth, so forces work in from all sides work and determine our ether body.' (GA 224, p. 94). In relation to the reintegration of the etheric body into the cosmic context after death, compare Selg, *Rudolf Steiners Totengedenken*. pp. 126ff.
29   GA 96, p. 216.
30   This and the following quote, GA 96, pp. 214f.
31   GA 97, p. 113.

32 GA 96, pp. 218f.

33 GA 148, p. 251.

34 GA 97, pp. 114f.

35 Goltz *(Das Gebet in der ältesten Christenheit,* p. 43) stated that 'In the way the Lord spoke these words before the disciples, they were not as yet a prayer, but merely an instruction for praying. They were intended to and could become prayer insofar as they were earnestly repeated.'

36 In questions after a lecture in Oslo in 1912, Rudolf Steiner said that the Lord's Prayer contains the 'originating powers of the human being'. Notes by Camille Wandrey of a question-and-answer session with Rudolf Steiner on the Lord's Prayer. Rudolf Steiner Archive, Dornach.

37 GA 96, p. 217.

38 GA 131. In relation to Steiner's view of the phantom and resurrection body, see Prokofieff, *The Mystery of the Resurrection,* pp. 69ff.

39 GA 343, p. 151.

40 See Note 48 of Ch. 3.

41 GA 343, p. 152.

42 GA 343, p. 152.

43 See Selg, *Vom Logos menschlicher Physis,* Vol. 2, pp. 569ff.

44 GA 293, p. 126.

45 GA 191, p. 171.

46 Frieling, *Der erneuerte christliche Gottesdienst,* p. 103. 'In the Lord's Prayer, the first phrase does not really refer to future development but to the beginning, the origin of things. The Lord's Prayer is really conceived as time measure, and this therefore relates to the beginning ...' (GA 343, p. 630).

47 This, and the following quotes are from GA 343, pp. 151f, 152f, 153, 154, 153f.

48 GA 343, pp. 154f.

49 The wording of Rudolf Steiner's comments in Dornach on the question of debt or guilt, and forgiveness, especially in relation to injury done to the divine, spiritual realm as a 'being' (the higher being of one's own existence) suggests in my view – as does the whole tone and style – that the formulation of the fifth petition of the Esoteric Lord's Prayer is attributable to Rudolf Steiner. Nevertheless (see also Note 54 of Ch. 1), the fact remains that the fifth petition does not appear in the standard transcripts of the 'Esoteric Lord's Prayer' or not in association with the original wording. It was therefore very probably a later addition. That it does not figure is very probably due to the real secret of this esoteric transcript, which was more than, and different from, a translation.

50 GA 343, p. 155f.

51 Frieling, *Der erneuerte christliche Gottesdienst,* p. 115.

52 In relation to this, see for instance, GA 130 (lecture of Dec 2, 1911) and GA 131 (lecture of Oct 14, 1911).

53 GA 343, p. 155.

54 Selg, *The Figure of Christ.* See also Wiesberger, *Rudolf Steiners esoterische Lehrtätigkeit,* pp. 90–96.

55 Frieling, *Der erneuerte christliche Gottesdienst,* p. 117.

56 In relation to the significance of the *human form* in anthroposophy, see Hella Wiesberger's exposition in *Beiträge zur Rudolf Steiner Gesamtausgabe.* No. 37/38, 1972, pp. 87–91.

57 GA 342, pp. 193ff.

58 Rittelmeyer, *Das Vaterunser,* p. 154f.

59 Compare Becker & Peter, *Das Heilige Vaterunser,* p. 4.

60 Selg, *Christus und die Jünger,* pp. 48ff, 103ff.

Bibliography

Works by Rudolf Steiner

GA volumes refer to the Collected Works (Gesamtausgabe) of Rudolf Steiner, all published by Rudolf Steiner Verlag, Dornach, Switzerland. Where there are recent translations into English these are added.

GA 9 *Theosophie* (1904), 32nd edition, 2003 *(Theosophy: An Introduction to the Spiritual Process in Human Life and the Cosmos,* Anthroposophic Press, USA 1994).

GA 26 *Anthroposophische Leitsätze* (1924/25), 10th edition, 1998 *(Anthroposophical Leading Thoughts: Anthroposophy as a Path of Knowledge,* Rudolf Steiner Press, UK 1998).

GA 27 *Grundlegendes für eine Erweiterung der Heilkunst nach geisteswissenschaftlichen Erkenntnissen* (1925), 7th edition, 1991 *(Fundamentals of Therapy: An Extension of the Art of Healing through Spiritual-Scientific Knowledge,* Mercury Press, USA 2010).

GA 28 *Mein Lebensgang* (1923 1925); 9th edition, 2000 *(Autobiography: Chapters in the Course of my Life,* SteinerBooks, USA 2006).

GA 39 *Briefe,* vol. II (1890 1925), 2nd edition, 1987.

GA 59 *Metamorphosen des Seelenlebens II* (1910), 1st edition, 1984 *(Metamorphoses of the Soul: Paths of Experience,* Vol. 2, Rudolf Steiner Press, UK 1983).

GA 93a *Grundelemente der Esoterik* (1905), 3rd edition 1987 *(Foundations of Esotericism,* Rudolf Steiner Press, UK 1983).

GA 96 *Ursprungsimpulse der Geisteswissenschaft* (1906/07), 2nd edition, 1989 *(Original Impulses for the Science of the Spirit,* Completion Press, Queensland, Australia 2001).

GA 97 *Das christliche Mysterium* (1906/07), 3rd edition, 1998 *(The Christian Mystery,* Completion Press, Queensland, Australia 2001).

GA 99 *Die Theosophie des Rosenkreuzers* (1907), 7th edition, 1985 *(Rosicrucians Wisdom: An Introduction,* Rudolf Steiner Press, UK 2010).

GA 100 *Menschheitsentwicklung und Christus Erkenntnis* (1907), 3rd edition, 2006.

GA 110 *Geistige Hierarchien und ihre Widerspiegelung in der physischen Welt* (1909), 7th edition, 1991 *(The Spiritual Hierarchies and the Physical World: Zodiac, Planets and Cosmos,* SteinerBooks, USA 2008).

GA 123 *Das Matthäus Evangelium* (1910), 7th edition, 1988 *(According to Matthew,* Anthroposophic Press, USA 2003).

GA 130 *Das esoterische Christentum und die geistige Führung der Menschheit* (1911/1912), 4th edition, 1995 *(Esoteric Christianity and the Mission of Christian Rosenkreutz,* Rudolf Steiner Press, UK 2005).

GA 131 *Von Jesus zu Christus* (1911), 7th edition, 1988 *(From Jesus to Christ,* Rudolf Steiner Press, UK 1973).

GA 132 *Die Evolution vom Gesichtspunkt des Wahrhaftigen* (1911), 7th edition, 1999 *(Inner Experiences of Evolution,* SteinerBooks, USA 2008).

GA 148 *Aus der Akasha* Chronik (1913/14), 5th edition, 1992 *(The Fifth Gospel,* Rudolf Steiner Press, UK 1995).

GA 167 *Gegenwärtiges und Vergangenes im Menschengeiste* (1916), 2nd edition, 1962.

GA 175 *Bausteine zu einer Erkenntnis des Mysteriums von Golgotha* (1917), 3rd edition, 1996.

GA 191 *Soziales Verständnis aus geisteswissenschaftlicher Erkenntnis* (1919), 3rd edition, 1989.

GA 196 *Geistige und soziale Wandlungen in der Menschheitsentwicklung* (1920), 2nd edition, 1992 *(What is Necessary in These Urgent Times,* SteinerBooks, USA 2010).

GA 203 *Die Verantwortung des Menschen für die Weltentwickelung durch seinen geistigen Zusammenhang mit dem Erdplaneten und der Sternenwelt* (1921), 2nd edition, 1989.

GA 211 *Das Sonnenmysterium und das Mysterium von Tod und Auferstehung* (1922), 3rd edition, 2006 *(The Sun Mystery and the Mystery of Death and Resurrection,* SteinerBooks, USA 2006).

GA 213 *Menschenfragen und Weltenantworten* (1922), 2nd edition, 1987.

GA 224 *Die menschliche Seele in ihrem Zusammenhang mit den göttlichengeistigen Individualitäten* (1923), 3rd edition, 1992.

GA 240 *Esoterische Betrachtungen karmischer Zusammenhänge.* Vol. VI (1924), 5th edition, 1992 (mostly in *Karmic Relationships,* Vol.8, Rudolf Steiner Press, UK 1975).

GA 258 *Die Geschichte und die Bedingungen der anthroposophischen Bewegung im Verhältnis zur Anthroposophischen Gesellschaft* (1923), 3rd edition, 1981.

GA 262 Rudolf Steiner / Marie Steiner von Sivers, *Briefwechsel und Dokumente* (1921 1925), 2nd edition, 2002 *(Correspondence and Documents 1901–1925,* Anthroposophic Press, USA 1988).

GA 264 *Zur Geschichte und aus den Inhalten der ersten Abteilung der Esoterischen Schule* (1904 1914), 2nd edition, 1996 *(From the History and Contents of the First Section of the Esoteric School 1904–1914,* SteinerBooks, USA 2007.

GA 266/1 *Aus den Inhalten der esoterischen Stunden.* Vol. 1 (1904–1909), 2nd edition, 2007 *(Esoteric Lessons: From the Esoteric School,* Vol. 1, SteinerBooks, USA 2011).

GA 266/2 *Aus den Inhalten der esoterischen Stunden.* Vol. 2 (1910–1912), 1st edition, 1996 *(Esoteric Lessons: From the Esoteric School,* Vol. 2, SteinerBooks, USA 2011).

GA 293 *Allgemeine Menschenkunde als Grundlage der Pädagogik* (1919), 9th edition, 1992 *(The Foundations of Human Experience,* Anthroposophic Press, USA 1996).

GA 300a *Konferenzen mit den Lehrern der Freien Waldorfschule.* Vol. 1 (1919–1921), 2nd edition, 1995 *(Faculty Meetings with Rudolf Steiner,* Vol. 1, Anthroposophic Press, USA 1998).

GA 325 *Die Naturwissenschaft und die weltgeschichtliche Entwickelung der Menschheit seit dem Altertum* (1921), 2nd edition, 1989.

GA 342 *Vorträge über christlich religiöses Wirken,* Vol. 1 (1921), 1st edition, 1993 *(First Steps in Christian Religious Renewal,* SteinerBooks, USA 2010.

GA 343 *Vorträge über christlich religiöses Wirken,* Vol. 2 (1921), 1st edition, 1993.

GA 344 *Vorträge über christlich religiöses Wirken,* Vol. 3 (1921), 1st edition, 1994.

GA 351 *Mensch und Welt. Das Wirken des Geistes in der Natur* (1923), 4th edition, 1988.

GA 353 *Die Geschichte der Menschheit und die Weltanschauungen der Kulturvölker* (1924), 2nd edition, 1988 *(From Beetroot to Buddhism,* Rudolf Steiner Press, UK 1999.

Steiner, *Selbstzeugnisse. Autobiographische Dokumente,* ed. Walter Kugler. Dornach 2007.

Other Authors

Aquinas, Thomas, *Das Vaterunser* in Hoffmann, Fritz and Kulok, Alfred (ed.), *Thomas von Aquin als Seelsorger. Drei kleine Werke.* Leipzig 1988.

Althoff, Karl Friedrich, *Das Vaterunser. Die Wortgestalt des Menschheitsgebetes auf ihrem Weg durch die Kulturen der Völker,* Stuttgart 1978.

Becker, Karl and Peter, Maria, *Das Heilige Vaterunser,* Freiburg 1951.

Bock, Emil, *Das Evangelium: Betrachtungen zum neuen Testament,* Stuttgart 1995 *(Studies in the Gospels,* (2 vols.) Floris Books, 2009, 2011.

—, *The Life and Times of Rudolf Steiner: Volume 1 and Volume 2,* Floris Books 2022.

Bock, Johann Peter, *Die Brotbitte des Vaterunsers,* Paderborn 1911.

Cullmann, Oscar, *Urchristentum und Gottesdienst,* Zurich 1950 *(Early Christian Worship,* SCM Press, London 1953).

—, *Das Gebet im neuen Testament,* Tübingen 1994 *Prayer in the New Testament,* Augsburg Fortress, Minneapolis 1995.

Debus, Michael & Kacer, Gundhild, *Das Handeln im Umkreis des Todes: Fragen zur Bestattung,* Stuttgart 1996.

Dibelius, Otto, *Das Vaterunser: Umrisse zu einer Geschichte des Gebetes in der alten und mittleren Kirche,* Giessen 1903.

Emmichoven, Emanuel Zeylmans van, *Die Erkraftung des Herzens. Eine Mysterienschulung der Gegenwart. Rudolf Steiners Anleitungen für Ita Wegman.* Arlesheim 2009 *(Who was Ita Wegman?* Vol. 4, Mercury Press, USA 2013).

—, *Wer war Ita Wegman: Eine Dokumentation*, 3 vols. Heidelberg 1992 *(Who was Ita Wegman?* Vol. 1–3, Mercury Press, USA 1995, 2005).

Emmichoven, Willem Zeylmans van, *Der Grundstein*, Stuttgart 1990 *(The Foundation Stone,* Temple Lodge Press 2002).

Frieling, Rudolf, *Gesammelte Schriften zum Alten und Neuen Testament*, 3 vols. Stuttgart 1986 (Some parts are in *The Complete Old Testament Studies,* Floris Books 2022, and *The Complete New Testament Studies,* Floris Books 2022).

—, *Der erneuerte christliche Gottesdienst: Beiträge zu seinem Verständnis,* Hannover 2002.

Furberg, Ingemar, *Das Pater Noster in der Messe*, Lund 1968.

Gädeke, Rudolf F. *Die Gründer der Christengemeinschaft: Ein Schicksalsnetz,* Dornach 1992.

Gädeke, Wolfgang, *Anthroposophie und die Fortbildung der Religion*, Flensburg 1990.

Goltz, Eduard von der, *Das Gebet in der ältesten Christenheit*, Leipzig 1901.

Guardini, Romano, *Das Gebet des Herrn*, Mainz 1934.

Heidenreich, Alfred, *Growing Point, The Story of the Foundation of the Christian Community,* Floris Books 1979.

Heydebrand, Caroline von (ed.), *Rudolf Steiner in der Waldorfschule*, Stuttgart 1927.

Jungmann, Josef Andreas, *Missarum sollemnia: Eine genetische Erklärung der römischen Messe*, 2 vols. Vienna 1948.

—, *Christliches Beten im Wandel und Bestand*, Freiburg 1991.

Kelber, Wilhelm, 'Christus im Vaterunser' In: Rau, Christoph, *Wege zum Beten,* Stuttgart 1985.

Kisseleff, Tatyana, *Eurythmische Arbeit mit Rudolf Steiner,* Dornach 1982.

Krause-Zimmer, Hella, *Christian Rosenkreutz: Die Inkarnationen*, Dornach 2009.

Lindenberg, Christoph, *Individualismus und offenbare Religion: Rudolf Steiners Zugang zum Christentum,* Stuttgart 1995.

Meyer, Thomas, *Rudolf Steiners 'eigenste Mission'. Ursprung und Aktualität geisteswissenschaftlicher Karmaforschung*, Basel 2009 *(Rudolf Steiner's Core Mission: The Birth and Development of Spiritual Scientific Karma Research,* Temple Lodge Press 2010).

Origen, *Über das Beten*, Ed. Wilhelm Maas, Stuttgart 1997.

Paracelsus, *Mahl des Herrn und Auslegung des Vaterunsers*, Ed. Gerhard Degeller, Dornach 1993.

Poeppig, Fred, *Das Vaterunser als Menschheits- und Erkenntnisgebet*, Basel 1956.

Prokofieff, Sergei O. *Das Mysterium der Auferstehung im Lichte der Anthroposophie*, Stuttgart 2008 *(The Mystery of the Resurrection in the Light of Anthroposophy,* Temple Lodge Press 2010).

Rau, Christoph, *Wege zum Beten*, Stuttgart 1985.

Rittelmeyer, Friedrich, *Rudolf Steiner Enters my Life,* Floris Books 2013.

—, *Das Vaterunser: Ein Weg zur Menschwerdung,* Stuttgart 1998 *(The Lord's*

Prayer, Macmillan 1931).

Schroeder, Hans Werner, *Das Gebet: Übung und Erfahrung*, Stuttgart 1977.

Selg, Peter, *Die Arbeit des Einzelnen und der Geist der Gemeinschaft. Rudolf Steiner und das 'Soziale Hauptgesetz'*. Dornach 2007 *(Rudolf Steiner and the Fundamental Social Law*, SteinerBooks, USA 2011).

—, *Christus und die Jünger: Vom Schicksal der inneren Gemeinschaft*, Arlesheim 2009 *(Christ and the Disciples: The Destiny of an Inner Community*, SteinerBooks, USA 2012).

—, *Das Ereignis der Jordantaufe: Epiphanias im Urchristentum und in der Anthroposophie Rudolf Steiners*, Stuttgart 2008.

—, *Die Gestalt Christi: Rudolf Steiner und die geistige Intention des zentralen Goetheanum-Kunstwerkes*, Arlesheim 2008 *(The Figure of Christ: Rudolf Steiner and the Spiritual Intention Behind the Goetheanum's Central Work of Art*, Temple Lodge Press 2009).

—, *'Ich bleibe bei Ihnen.' Rudolf Steiner und Ita Wegman: München, Pfingsten 1907 – Dornach, 1923-1925*, Stuttgart 2007.

—, *Mysterium cordis. Studien zur sakramentalen Physiologie des Herzorganes – Thomas von Aquin – Rudolf Steiner*. Dornach 2006 *(The Mystery of the Heart: Studies in Spiritual Physiology*, SteinerBooks, USA 2012).

—, *Rudolf Steiner und das Fünfte Evangelium: Eine Studie*, Dornach 2010 *(Rudolf Steiner and the Fifth Gospel*, SteinerBooks, USA 2010).

—, *Rudolf Steiners Totengedenken:. Die Verstorbenen, der Dornacher Bau und die Anthroposophische Gesellschaft*, Arlesheim 2008 *The Path of the Soul after Death*, SteinerBooks, USA 2011).

—, *Vom Logos menschlicher Physis. Die Entfaltung einer anthroposophischen Humanphysiologie im Werk Rudolf Steiners*, 2 vols. Dornach 2006.

Steiner-von Sivers, Marie, 'Wendepunkte des Geisteslebens' in *Die Anthroposophie Rudolf Steiners: Gesammelte Schriften I*, Dornach 1967.

Stritzky, Maria Barbara von, *Studien zur Überlieferung und Interpretation des Vaterunsers in der frühchristlichen Literatur*, Müster 1989.

Wagner, Reinhard, *Die unbekannten Jahre Jesu*, Stuttgart 1995.

Wegman, Ita, *An die Freunde*, Arlesheim 1986 (Selections in *Ita Wegman: Esoteric Studies*, Temple Lodge Press 2013).

—, *Erinnerung an Rudolf Steiner*, Arlesheim 2011.

Wiesberger, Hella, *Marie Steiner-von Sivers: Ein Leben für die Anthroposophie*, Dornach 1989.

—, *Rudolf Steiners esoterische Lehrtätigkeit: Wahrhaftigkeit, Kontinuität, Neugestaltung*, Dornach 1997.

Zeylmans van Emmichoven *see* Emmichoven.

Ita Wegman Institute
for Basic Research into Anthroposophy

Pfeffinger Weg 1A 4144 Arlesheim, Switzerland
www.wegmaninstitute.ch

The Ita Wegman Institute for Basic Research into Anthroposophy is a non-profit research and teaching organisation. It undertakes basic research into the lifework of Dr Rudolf Steiner (1861–1925) and the application of Anthroposophy in specific areas of life, especially medicine, education, and curative education. Work carried out by the Institute is supported by a number of foundations and organizations and an international group of friends and supporters. The Director of the Institute is Prof Dr Peter Selg.

Milton Keynes UK
Ingram Content Group UK Ltd.
UKHW022349041223
433767UK00009B/470